CW00670416

IT MUST BE LOVE

A FARCICAL COMEDY IN TWO ACTS

RAYMOND HOPKINS

HANBURY PLAYS

KEEPER'S LODGE • BROUGHTON GREEN
DROITWICH • WORCESTERSHIRE • WR9 7EE

BY THE SAME AUTHOR:
LOVE BEGINS AT FIFTY

IT MUST BE LOVE
FIRST PUBLISHED 2001
by
HANBURY PLAYS
Keeper's Lodge Broughton Green
Droitwich Worcestershire WR9 7EE

ISBN:- 185205 257 0

Copyright © Raymond Hopkins 2000

The author of this play, Raymond Hopkins, is donating his share of the proceeds to
MULTIPLE SCLEROSIS RESEARCH

CAST IN ORDER OF APPEARANCE

JOHN TAYLOR — About forty-eight. Lets the world go by, henpecked by his wife, loves gardening. Hard worker.

ANNE TAYLOR — About forty-five. Runs the family, but does not like to be put under pressure. Smartly dressed.

JASON TAYLOR — About twenty-five. Only child of John and Anne Taylor. Down to earth, a quiet, deep thinking, romantic person.

STELLA PARSONS — About fifty. Jumped-up snob, plenty of money, but in a loveless marriage. Trying to find a man who will give her affection.

LUCINDA PARSONS — About twenty-five. Only daughter of Stella and Reg Parsons. Emotional wreck, talks with a lisp, has been dominated by her mum. Does not make the best of herself until Act II, Scene II. Then she is transformed. She loses her lisp and looks lovely.

FRED STUBBLE — About sixty-eight. Reasonably well educated. A ladies' man, full of life and is a real character. Acts like a man twenty years younger.

JULIE HEMMINGS — About twenty-two. From poor background. Pretty girl who is kind and considerate.

CHRIS TUCKER — About twenty-five. Quick thinker. Jack-the-lad, anything goes, lives for today. Jason's best friend.

SID BLUNSDEN — About forty-five. Big thinker, full of flannel. Married, without children. Runs his own video recording business.

ALF PRATT — About thirty-five. Dishevelled nerd, who talks out of the back of his head. Lodges with Sid and his wife. Helps with Sid's video business.

REV. ALAN STEVENS — Chris in dog collar with disguise. Suggest beard, glasses, wig or false teeth. Also use different voice and a fictitious actor's name in programme.

NOTES

(1) The whole plot of the play depends on Chris not being recognisable as the Rev. Alan Stevens.

(2) In Act I, Scene I, Anne and Stella must be wearing similar coloured clothes.

THE ACTION TAKES PLACE IN A SMALL TOWN IN THE MIDLANDS.
IT IS SET IN THE LOUNGE OF THE TAYLORS' SEMI-DETACHED
HOUSE. IT IS LATE SPRING – THE PRESENT DAY

ACT I

Scene One – Saturday morning – one week before the wedding

Scene Two – The following Monday – late afternoon

ACT II

Scene One – The following Wednesday – late afternoon

Scene Two – The following Sunday morning

ACT 1

ꙮ Scene I ꙮ

(As the curtain rises, John is sitting in a chair, reading a newspaper. The phone starts to ring. John answers it)

JOHN   Hello ... hello, Sandra ... yes ... no ... yes ...

(John holds the phone away from his ear and moves his head from side to side, pretending to talk. Anne enters from kitchen, unseen by John)

ANNE   What are you doing?

JOHN   Ahh ... *(John faces Anne)* Nothing ... it's your sister. *(Puts hand over phone)* She's upset about the wedding.

(John hands over phone. Anne glares at him. John sits down and reads paper)

ANNE   Hello, Sandra ... pardon? ... Look, I agree with you, your daughter should have been asked. Oh, don't be like that ... *(John looks up)* ... just calm down ... *(John reads paper)* ... Sandra ... Sandra ... Sandra? *(Anne puts phone down.)*

                 I can't believe it, she's hung up. *(Pause)* They're not coming to the wedding.

JOHN   *(Looking up from paper)* Why not?

ANNE   Because Jennifer wasn't asked to be a bridesmaid. *(Pause)* Mind you it's not fair, the six bridesmaids are all from the other side.

JOHN   You make it sound as if they've risen from the dead.

ANNE   Don't be stupid, you know what I mean. What am I going to do?

JOHN   Phone her back and say she can be a bridesmaid.

ANNE   The wedding's next week and Jennifer hasn't got a dress.

JOHN   She could wear that blue one she had for her birthday.

ANNE   Everyone else'll be in *pink*. If she wears blue she'll stand out like a ballet dancer working on a building site.

JOHN   You should have sorted all this out before.

ANNE	Lucinda and her mum had chosen all the bridesmaids before I'd realised.
JOHN	It's our son that's getting married. Surely we can pick one.

(Phone rings)

| ANNE | This phone's just not stopped. *(Anne picks up phone, John reads paper)* Hello ... hello, Jack ... I don't know ... can't you take it back? ... Oh I see ... well you did have the wedding list ... bye. |

(Anne puts down phone. John looks up from paper)

Jack's found out someone else has bought a toaster.

| JOHN | He'll have to go back to the shop and change it. |
| ANNE | He didn't buy it from a shop, he got it from a car boot sale. *(Pause)* This wedding's getting too much for me. It's been one crisis after another. |

(Phone rings)

JOHN	That'll be Jack again. He bought that cheap phone which keeps going into redial mode.
ANNE	*(Getting cross)* I've just about had enough. *(Picking up phone)* You've done it again, you pillock! ... Oh, hello, Vicar ... yes, certainly ... we're really looking forward to the wedding ... see you soon ... bye. *(Anne puts down phone)* I think I've just ruined my chances of seeing the pearly gates.
JOHN	What did the Reverend Hall want?
ANNE	He's calling round Monday to see Jason and Lucinda. *(Pause)* Where's my list? *(Anne looks around room)*
JOHN	Your whole life revolves around a list of jobs on a piece of paper.
ANNE	That's because although I can remember what I did forty years ago, I haven't a clue what happened yesterday.
JOHN	That's nothing to worry about. *(Pause)* It's just part of the ageing process.
ANNE	Watch it. *(Anne picks up clipboard with A4 sheet on it)* Ah, here we are. *(Reading from list)* You've got to see your friends about videoing the wedding.
JOHN	There's no panic, I'll do that tomorrow.
ANNE	*(Looks back at list)* I've got to ring the florist about our buttonholes.
JOHN	Don't bother to get me one. I've got some roses in the garden.
ANNE	Don't be stupid, you're the bridegroom's father. You'll have one from the florist like everyone else. *(Looking back at list)* I've got so much to do, it's ridiculous.
JOHN	Calm down or you'll have one of your power surges.

6

ANNE	Flippant remarks about my hot flushes are in poor taste.
JOHN	I've never seen you so uptight.
ANNE	It's all right for you sitting there oblivious of everything.
JOHN	Weddings are overrated. They're just an excuse for lots of sad people to try and outdo each other in some glorified fashion parade.
ANNE	The only sad person is you. You're such a skinflint you'd have the bride arriving on a pushbike, and the reception at *Sloppy Sam's Snack Bar*. *(Phone rings)* You can get that.
JOHN	*(Picking up phone)* Hello ... Oh right, that's good ... So it's well rotted ... Thank you. *(John puts down the phone)* They're delivering my manure within the next few days.
ANNE	If you put as much effort into your son's wedding as you do that wretched garden you'd ... *(Looking at her list)* I've written down "make love."
JOHN	Now that is good news. It's not my birthday is it?
ANNE	It's all right ... I remember what it is now.
JOHN	I hope you do. Come on, let's go for it before you have another amnesia attack. *(John holds out his hand and heads for hall exit)*
ANNE	Come back here, Romeo. *(Pause)* You've got to have a talk to your son about what to do in bed.
	(John walks back into room)
JOHN	Anne, the age of innocence has gone, it's free love for all now.
ANNE	Best to be on the safe side. Just make sure he knows what goes where.
JOHN	You've only got to turn the telly on, open a magazine, or go to the cinema. It's reached epidemic proportions.
ANNE	We don't want his honeymoon to be like ours. That was a total disaster.
JOHN	You said you wouldn't mention that again.
ANNE	We spent all night doing a jigsaw puzzle of a squirrel. At breakfast next morning, when you said you couldn't find your nuts, everybody laughed. *(Pause)* They didn't know you were on about a lost piece of puzzle.
JOHN	Perhaps we could get the vicar to explain what to do.
ANNE	Don't be stupid, that's not his job. *(Looking at list)* Now let me see. We've got Lucinda and her mum calling in to make the final arrangements.
JOHN	In that case I'll mow the lawns.

ANNE	Oh no you don't. You'll stay here and talk to Stella.
JOHN	I can't stand the woman. She's nothing but a jumped-up snob.
ANNE	I've got to admit she's going over the top with this wedding.
JOHN	It must have cost them at least fifty grand.
ANNE	And the rest. *(Pause)* I'll miss Jason when he moves out. *(Pause)* I might get a dog.
JOHN	Animals are a big responsibility. A dog's not just for Christmas.
ANNE	That's good, because summer's almost here. *(Pause)* It'll be a new interest in life, something for me to shower my affection on.

(John puts his arm around Anne)

JOHN	You can always shower your affection on me. Why have a dog when I'm here?
ANNE	Because I can put the dog in a kennel at night, when I want to get to sleep. *(John removes his arm from Anne)*
JOHN	Umm ... *(Pause)* I see your point.
ANNE	Have a think about it, and let me know.
JOHN	If we do get one, we'll call it *Randy*, just like its master!
ANNE	That's a laugh.
JOHN	I've got something in my right eye, would you have a look?
ANNE	*(Peering into John's eye)* I can't see anything, it's probably some down off that new quilt.
JOHN	It's really sore. I can't stop blinking.
ANNE	Don't make such a fuss, you big baby.

(Jason enters from hall)

Morning, darling, did you sleep well?

JASON	Not too bad, although I kept thinking about the wedding.
ANNE	I expect you'll be pleased when the big day's here.
JASON	I suppose so, although it all seems to be getting a bit out of hand.
JOHN	How long have you and Lucinda been courting?
JASON	What do you mean, courting?
JOHN	Good grief, I can't be that old, can I? How long have you two been going out together?

8

JASON	I'm not sure, she always seems to have been hanging around.
ANNE	You'd better not let Lucinda hear you say that.
JOHN	I'll put some toast on for your breakfast. *(Pause)* Come on, Randy. WALKIES!

(John exits to kitchen, pretending to lead a dog)

JASON	Is Dad feeling all right?
ANNE	Yes, we've been talking about getting a dog.
JASON	Oh, I see. *(Pause)* Just before your wedding, did you have any doubts?
ANNE	I think everybody does. After all it's a big decision.
JASON	How do you know when you're in love?
ANNE	It's no good asking me; I'm married.
JASON	But that's just what I mean. How do you know if you've chosen the right person?
ANNE	What's brought all this on? Don't tell me you and Lucinda have had a row?
JASON	No. It's just me. Last minute nerves and all that.
ANNE	Oh, that's good. *(Pause)* How are you getting on with Lucinda's mum?
JASON	Absolutely fine *(Pause)* when she's not around.
ANNE	Jason, you're talking about your future mother-in-law.
JASON	I'll tell you something. She's a man-eater.
ANNE	What, Stella? I can't believe that.
JASON	It's true. Her husband's lost interest, so she's looking elsewhere.
ANNE	Goodness, I'd never have thought that of her.
JASON	I think she's trying to re-live her lost youth.
ANNE	Aren't we all?

(John enters from kitchen)

JOHN	It's in the toaster. *(Doorbell rings)* My eye's still sore.

(John exits to hall rubbing his eye)

(Off) Hello, Stella, Lucinda. Come in.

STELLA	*(Off)* Hello, John. *(Lucinda, Stella, John enter. Stella is carrying a large picture, which she puts on sideboard)* Well, only one week before my little Lucinda becomes the bride of the year. Hello, Jason. *(Pinches his cheek)* You'll soon be calling me Mother.
JASON	I can't wait.

9

LUCINDA	Mummy, do you think my wedding photos will be in all the local papers?
STELLA	Of course they will, darling. I expect they'll be on the front page.
LUCINDA	That's good. *(Pause)* Kim Swanson was interviewed by the local radio on her wedding day.
STELLA	Was she? I'll phone and make sure they interview you.
JASON	We don't want too much publicity.
STELLA	Don't be silly. My Lucinda's going to have the full works.
JOHN	*(Aside)* I wish someone would give you the full works.
STELLA	We can't stop long. Lucinda's got her final dress fitting.
LUCINDA	I hope they've sewn the sequins on, and lengthened the train.
STELLA	Don't worry your pretty little head, darling, Mummy will sort it all out.
ANNE	Are you pleased with the dress, Lucinda?
LUCINDA	I think it's ...
STELLA	The last time she tried it on, I just wept and wept buckets of tears.
JOHN	Was it that bad?
STELLA	She looked so beautiful. Just like a princess.
JOHN	When I tried my wedding suit on I wept. I couldn't believe it was costing so much.
LUCINDA	I hope it won't rain on my wedding day.
STELLA	*(Looking up)* It had better not, or I shall want to know the reason why.
JOHN	My garden could do with a good soaking. The spuds are no bigger than marbles.
STELLA	Your potatoes'll have to wait. I've ordered fine weather for Saturday.
LUCINDA	I won't be able to see you tonight, Jason. I've got a beautician and hair stylist calling round for a consultation.
JOHN	*(Aside)* Perhaps they can work a miracle on your mum.
ANNE	What are you muttering about, John?
JOHN	I just said that could be a lot of fun.
STELLA	We've got a top hairdresser. He's creating a unique style just for my Lucy Lou.
ANNE	I'm sure you'll look absolutely beautiful.
STELLA	Now we must sort out the church service ...

JOHN	I'll just go and mow the lawns.
JASON	My toast should be ready. *(Anne glares at John)*
STELLA	That's right, off you pop and leave us girls to make the final arrangements.

(Jason and John exit to kitchen)

Now, where were we? Oh yes, last night I had a nightmare about choirboys.

ANNE	Choirboys?
STELLA	*(Stella goes into a panic)* They were all suffering from laryngitis and couldn't sing a note.
ANNE	Oh dear, how awful.
STELLA	I phoned the Reverend Hall this morning and told him to bring some spare ones along.
LUCINDA	Would it be all right if I got myself a cold drink? I'm feeling a bit flushed.
STELLA	Promise Mummy you're not going to be ill. *(Stella puts her hand on Lucinda's forehead)* Have you got a fever?
LUCINDA	I did sneeze four times yesterday.
STELLA	Oh no! When we get home I'll get the doctor to call round.
LUCINDA	All right, Mummy. I'll go and have a chat to Jason.
STELLA	Don't get cold, Lucy Lou.

(Lucinda exits to kitchen)

That's all I need. Now where was I? Oh, yes. I've told the hire company I want more cars.

ANNE	But we've already got three, and a horse and carriage. We could transport a rugby team.
STELLA	I've changed it to five cars, plus the horse and carriage.
ANNE	I don't really see the point.
STELLA	Best to be on the safe side. In any case, that Mrs Ferguson had four cars for her daughter's wedding.
ANNE	I've just had a phone call from my sister. They're not coming to the wedding.
STELLA	Tell me it isn't because they feel inferior to my family.
ANNE	Certainly not. It's because her daughter wasn't asked to be a bridesmaid.
STELLA	I'm sure we can work something out.

11

ANNE	Thank you so much. It's just that she's always wanted to be a bridesmaid, and I feel ….
STELLA	I've got it. *(Looking thoughtful)* The guests will need directing to the loos. *(Looking pleased)* Is that a possibility?
ANNE	My niece isn't going to be a lavatory attendant.
STELLA	Oh, well, it was just a thought.
ANNE	I'm not very happy about this. After all, she is my sister.
STELLA	I completely understand how you feel. *(Pause)* We can choose our friends, but we can't choose family.
ANNE	So what am I going to tell Sandra?
STELLA	Tell her not to worry, we'll soon fill their seats at the reception.
ANNE	That's no good. This has put me into an impossible position.
STELLA	Did I tell you that I've invited the mayor and his wife?
ANNE	I didn't realise you knew them.
STELLA	I don't, but it all helps to give the occasion that certain something. They've accepted, and he's told me he'll be wearing his robe and chains.
ANNE	Oh, that'll be nice for him.
STELLA	He's already given me his wedding present. *(Stella picks up the large abstract picture from sideboard. The picture is random-coloured lines, squiggles, and circles)* Have a look at this. *(Stella hands picture to Anne)* What do you think?
ANNE	*(Holding picture upside-down and staring at it)* It looks a bit rude to me.
STELLA	You've got it upside-down. *(Anne turns picture up the right way)* He was in an abstract mood when he painted this. It's called *Forgotten Dreams*.
ANNE	*(Looking vague)* It's certainly different.
STELLA	*(Snatching picture back)* One's got to be in tune with abstract art, to experience its hidden depths.
ANNE	If you say so. *(Stella puts the picture back onto the sideboard)*
STELLA	I've just had my final meeting with the wedding co-ordinator. I've told him if he doesn't get it right, his job's on the line.
ANNE	I wouldn't want to be in his shoes.
STELLA	The caterers are pushing their luck. They promised me a top chef from the London Academy, and now we've got some under chef from Luton airport.
ANNE	Are you sure we need seven courses? We'll be eating till midnight.

12

STELLA	Just leave it to me. Everything's organised. *(Pause)* My Reg got so excited last night. *(Pause)* It looked magnificent when it was lit up.
ANNE	I beg your pardon?
STELLA	The paddock. Reg put all the floodlights on.
ANNE	Oh, of course, we're having the reception in a marquee at your house.
STELLA	Well, I mean, with our ten acres, it seemed silly to go elsewhere. In any case, the orchestra insisted on perfect acoustics.
ANNE	We wouldn't want to upset the orchestra.
STELLA	By the way, are you sure these fellows will be all right videoing the wedding?
ANNE	Oh yes. John says they're very good.
STELLA	I'd much rather hire a professional firm. Money's no object.
ANNE	It's the only contribution our family's making. Don't worry, they'll be fine.
STELLA	We don't want any slip-ups. It's such an important event. Have you seen their credentials?
ANNE	No, I've not had that pleasure. *(Pause)* You don't think you're making too much of this wedding, do you?
STELLA	Whatever do you mean?
ANNE	We've got two-hundred and fifty guests. The whole town's been put on red alert. All police leave's been cancelled, and you're spending enough money to repaint the Millennium Dome.
STELLA	We can afford it. Reg's business is doing very well. Just leave it to me.
ANNE	If you're sure. I just thought that …
STELLA	Look, Lucinda's our only child. I shan't get another chance. I wanted more children, but Reg was always too busy with his road haulage company.

(John enters from kitchen)

JOHN	Where's the can of petrol for the mower?
ANNE	I don't know. *(Pause)* Oh, wait a minute, Bill next door borrowed it.
JOHN	That's just typical, everything we own, he borrows. I'll go and get it.
ANNE	No, you have a talk to Stella. I'll get it. I've got to see Margaret about a recipe.
JOHN	*(Pointedly)* Thanks a million.
STELLA	Of course, we have a gardener. He's so useful, I couldn't manage without him.

13

ANNE	Excuse me for a moment.

(Anne exits to hall)

JOHN	Reg must be doing well. I'm always seeing his lorries about.
STELLA	He's just taken on five more men. *(Getting excited)* One of them was an Eddie Stobart defector.
JOHN	Pardon?
STELLA	He got fed up wearing a tie to work. *(Pause)* Yesterday the bank manager took Reg out to lunch to discuss his stocks and shares.
JOHN	My bank manager's just had a word with me.
STELLA	What about, investments?
JOHN	No, my overdraft. Anybody would think they were short of money.
STELLA	Oh ... the only problem is, Reg is always working. We've become almost strangers.
JOHN	I suppose that's the price of running a successful business.
STELLA	I've told him we're not on this earth for long. You've got to have some fun.
JOHN	My motto's always been *'Enjoy each day as though it's your last'* 'cos one day it will be.
STELLA	I wish my husband had your outlook on life. *(Pause)* All work and no play makes Reg a dull boy.
JOHN	Still it's nice to be financially secure.
STELLA	I'd get more affection if I'd married a cash-dispenser machine.
JOHN	I suppose money doesn't buy happiness. It just eases the pain of life.
STELLA	Reg has never understood the emotional needs of a woman.
JOHN	There isn't a man living who understands the emotional needs of a woman.

(Doorbell rings, John exits to hall)

Excuse me. *(Off)* Hello, Fred, come in.

(John enters with Fred)

I don't think you've met Lucinda's mum, Stella Parsons. This is our friend Fred Stubble.

FRED	Pleased to meet you. *(They shake hands)*
STELLA	I'm sorry, but I can't remember if you're coming to the wedding, Mr Stubble.
FRED	You can call me Fred. All the girls do. And yes, I'll be there.

14

STELLA	That's good, and your wife?
FRED	I've lost her; she's gone.
STELLA	I am sorry, was it sudden?
FRED	You could say that. One morning I got up and found a note saying she'd run off with the milkman.
STELLA	Oh, dear, I should think you were devastated.
FRED	I was. *(Pause)* He hadn't left any milk.
STELLA	You must miss her dreadfully.
FRED	Yeah, I do, she was the only one who could work the washing machine.
STELLA	Have you heard from her since?
FRED	Not a word. I wouldn't have minded, but she took all me bottles of Guinness. Talking of drink, me throat's a bit dry.
JOHN	Sorry, Fred, would you like a drop of whisky?
FRED	That'll do nicely.
JOHN	Would you like a drink, Stella? We've got sherry, gin or whisky.

(John and Stella walk over to the drinks cabinet. Fred follows. He looks at Stella's legs)

FRED	*(Aside)* Ohh ... what a lovely pair of legs.
STELLA	Just a small sherry please. I've already had four glasses of wine with the mayor.
FRED	Make my whisky a large one.

(John pours out drinks)

JOHN	Cheers! *(They all hold up glasses)*
STELLA	Cheers!
FRED	

{STELLA / FRED brace} Cheers!

STELLA	To Lucinda and Jason.
FRED	And may they *enjoy the fruits of nature.*

(They all have a drink)

STELLA	Oh dear, that's gone straight to my head.
FRED	That's what comes of mixing your drinks.
STELLA	*(Hiccups loudly)* Pardon me! *(Stella has another long drink)* Would you top me up please? It's giving me a warm glow inside.
JOHN	Certainly.

15

(John fills Stella's glass)

STELLA   I don't normally indulge at this time of day. *(Taking another long drink)* Still, this is a special occasion.

FRED   I don't need a special occasion to have a drink.

(Stella is getting slightly tipsy)

STELLA   I could get used to this. *(Stella has another drink)* The trouble is, sherry works like an aphrodisiac on me.

FRED   *(Grabbing the sherry bottle)* Here, have another.

(Fred fills Stella's glass)

STELLA   *(Taking a sip)* I must be careful, two drinks and I'm anybody's.

JOHN   Don't worry. *(Aside)* I certainly won't be queuing up.

FRED   That's brought a bit of colour to your cheeks.

JOHN   *(Looking bored)* I hope Anne's not going to be long. I've got to mow the lawns.

(Stella walks over to some photos on the sideboard and bends over to look at them)

STELLA   When were these taken?

(John and Fred join Stella)

JOHN   *(Looking at photos)* About five years ago.

FRED   *(Looking at Stella's bottom.)* *(Aside)* Ahh ... Very nice indeed. *(Fred pats Stella's bottom, then moves away, leaving John standing by her)*

STELLA   Ohh! ... JOHN really, you do surprise me!

JOHN   Well, perhaps it was a bit longer then.

FRED   I just popped round to see if you need a hand behind the bar at the reception.

STELLA   That won't be necessary. We've hired bar staff.

JOHN   Fred used to work at the Nag's Head.

FRED   I used to have me own special drink called *Fred's Bomb*. *(Pause)* It was guaranteed to blow your brains out! *(Pause)* So, you won't be requiring my services?

STELLA   No thank you, Mr Stubble, I mean Fred. We'll be fine.

FRED   That's good, because I'll be able to get down to some serious drinking.

STELLA   I hope the service won't bring back any painful memories of your wedding.

FRED   No, I'll probably have a laugh at poor Jason getting tied down.

STELLA   *(To John)* Have I shown you our holiday photos?

16

JOHN	I expect so. I've watched every video and seen all the photos you've got.
STELLA	No, you won't have seen these. They only arrived yesterday.
JOHN	*(Aside)* Just my luck.
STELLA	Reginald and I were on holiday in our villa in the South of France.
FRED	They let it all hang out over there, don't they?
JOHN	What are you on about, Fred?

(Stella bends over sofa and rummages about in her handbag)

FRED	You can check what's on offer before signing your life away.

(Fred looks at Stella's bottom)

(Aside) Now that's what I like, a bit of beef on the bone.

(Fred stands by Stella and pats her bottom, then moves away, leaving John standing by her)

STELLA	Ohh …
JOHN	Don't worry if you can't find them.
STELLA	I've got them, you naughty boy. I really should be getting cross with you.
JOHN	Why? I didn't hide them.
STELLA	Obviously our little talk's got you thinking.

(Stella gives John a nudge)

FRED	Can I have a look?

(Stella hands round photos. John isn't interested. Fred has a good look)

STELLA	The trouble was, Reg spent all week on the phone to his business clients.

(Fred is studying the photos)

FRED	*(Aside)* That can join my page three collection.

(Fred puts a photo in his pocket)

JOHN	Thank you, very nice. *(John looks bored, he hands photos back)*
STELLA	There's one missing. *(Looking at John)* It's the one of me topless. I never realised, John.
JOHN	*(Oblivious of what's been going on)* Realised what?
STELLA	All the time our youngsters have been together, you've been hiding your inner feelings.
JOHN	*(Totally confused)* Sorry?

17

STELLA	Don't apologise, I'm just glad it's all out in the open. *(Pause)* Fred, be a dear, pop out to the Merc and get my mobile phone.

(Stella hands Fred car keys)

It's on the back seat.

(Fred exits to hall. Stella gets close to John)

Could I have another drink, please?

JOHN	Same again?
STELLA	Just a small one, I've got to be on my guard with you.

(John winks his sore eye several times)

There's no need to keep winking at me, John. I've already got the picture.

JOHN	Oh ... that's all down to a bit of fluff.
STELLA	You cheeky monkey.

(John picks up a bottle in one hand, and a glass in the other. He pours out a drink for Stella)

JOHN	Say when.
STELLA	That's lovely. *(Stella goes to take her drink, but knocks glass, spilling some over John's shirt)* Whoops ... I'm so sorry.
JOHN	Don't worry, it'll wash out.
STELLA	Let me sponge it now, then it won't stain.

(John is still holding bottle and glass. Stella gets her handkerchief and mops John's shirt)

JOHN	There's no need to go to all that trouble.
STELLA	*(Getting close to John)* It's a pleasure. Come here.
JOHN	*(Looking bored)* That'll be fine now.
STELLA	You've certainly got a good physique.
JOHN	That's all down to my gardening. It keeps me fit.
STELLA	I like a man with a firm body.

(Stella stops mopping shirt)

JOHN	I'm not one to let myself go. *(Glibly)* It keeps the girls interested.
STELLA	And to think I've never suspected a thing.
JOHN	What are you talking about?

(Stella now takes her drink)

18

STELLA	It's all dropping into place now. At the New Year's fancy dress party you were Robin Hood, and I was Maid Marion. I spent all night trying to keep my honour intact.
JOHN	I was just an innocent bystander.
STELLA	That's what they all say. *(Pause)* You playboy. I'd not had so much fun in ages.
JOHN	That Darth Vader was the real menace, poking his luminous rod everywhere. I'm convinced it was the Reverend Hall dressed up.
STELLA	It was five years ago when Reg lost his appetite, and put on loads of weight.
JOHN	Surely that's a physical impossibility?
STELLA	Well, it's a fact. He's sexually inactive, and fatter than Mr Blobby.
JOHN	*(Looking embarrassed)* I don't think you should be telling me this. Best to have a word with Reg.
STELLA	I've given up with him. Ours has become a marriage of convenience.
JOHN	Oh dear. *(Pause)* So what will you do when Lucinda moves out?
STELLA	I'll need a new interest in life. I'm not ready to be a frumpish, frigid, fifty-year-old.
JOHN	No, I'm sure you're not.
STELLA	I've just had an idea. Reg goes out Friday nights to his road haulage meeting. *(Looking vulnerable, Stella gets very close to John)* I get so bored on my own.
JOHN	*(Oblivious of Stella's advances)* You should invite a friend round for a few drinks.
STELLA	My thoughts exactly. We've obviously got the same problem; our partners have reached the mid-life switch off. I'm fed up with being starved of love and affection.
JOHN	*(Looking vague)* I think I'm missing something here.
STELLA	We both are. Have a think about it and let me know. I can be very discreet.

(Anne and Fred enter from hall, Stella moves away from John. Fred gives Stella her car keys and her mobile phone)

	Thank you, Fred.
ANNE	*(To John)* Here you are. *(Handing over petrol can)*
JOHN	There's nothing in here, it was full of petrol when he had it.
ANNE	I know. He said sorry but his car had run out, so he had to use it all.

JOHN	That's typical of him. The last time I loaned him a torch I didn't get it back until the batteries were dead.
ANNE	Don't make such a fuss.
JOHN	I'm going to put a lock on this can.
STELLA	*(To Anne)* Would you like to see Lucinda trying on her dress?
FRED	Yes, please, I'd love to.
STELLA	Actually, Mr Stubble, I was talking to Anne.
FRED	Oh sorry. *(Pause)* I wouldn't get in the way.
STELLA	It's a ladies' dress shop, full of half-naked women.
FRED	Is it? What are we waiting for? *(Fred walks to hall exit)*
JOHN	Leave it to the girls, Fred.
FRED	But I'm quite an expert when it comes to ladies' fashion.
STELLA	I'll just check it's ready. *(Stella dials number on mobile phone)* Hello, this is Stella Parsons. Could you tell me if my daughter's wedding dress is ready ... That's excellent ... we'll be round shortly ... bye.

(Anne bends down behind sofa and fiddles about with a castor)

ANNE	Everything all right?
STELLA	Yes, they say it's the most exquisite dress they've ever made. I'll probably burst into floods of tears the moment I see it.
JOHN	I'll get Lucinda. *(Aside)* I think I'm going to be sick.
ANNE	*(Still behind the sofa)* This castor's still faulty. I thought you were going to fix it.
JOHN	I'll do it tomorrow. *(John exits to kitchen)*
STELLA	When you buy from Harrods, you don't seem to get any problems. *(Pause)* Can we drop you off anywhere, Mr Stubble?
FRED	Are you sure you don't want my opinion on the dress?
STELLA	No, thank you, we'll manage. *(Anne stands up)*
FRED	In that case, would you drop me at the Nag's Head?
ANNE	Surely they won't be open at this time of day.
FRED	It's all right, I've got me own key.

(Lucinda and Jason enter from kitchen)

STELLA	Have you got your speech ready, Jason?
JASON	I'm no good at making speeches.

20

FRED	I've got some jokes that're guaranteed to make the girls wet their knickers.
ANNE	The Reverend Hall hasn't forgiven you for the ones you told at the Christmas party.
FRED	He hasn't got a sense of humour.
STELLA	Everybody ready? You'd better drive, Lucinda, I'm feeling a bit light-headed.
JASON	I'll come and see you off.

(Lucinda, Stella, Anne, Jason and Fred exit to hall)

STELLA	*(Off)* I've forgotten my handbag, *(Stella re-enters and knocks handbag off sofa arm, everything drops out. She goes behind sofa and picks up contents, John pokes his head round kitchen door. He thinks it is Anne behind the sofa)*
JOHN	You're not still fiddling with that castor. By the way, let's give it a try. *(Pause)* Don't forget, *Randy*'s the name. *(John exits to kitchen) (Off)* WALKIES.

(Stella picks up her handbag, stands up and smiles)

STELLA	*(To kitchen exit)* All right, Randy. See you Friday.

(Stella exits to hall. Car drives away. Jason enters. He puts on a tape of romantic music. He sits on chair and reads paper. The door bell rings. Jason exits to hall)

JULIE	*(Off)* Hello, I'm from 'Pinks' the florist. We're supplying the flowers for your wedding.
JASON	*(Off)* Really? You'd better come in. *(Jason and Julie enter room)*
JULIE	I've called to sort out what buttonholes you require?

(Jason turns music down low)

That's one of my favourite songs.

JASON	What a coincidence. It's my favourite too.
JULIE	I was going to phone, but it seemed easier to pop in and show you what I've got.
JASON	I'm glad you did. *(Pause)* I haven't seen you before.
JULIE	I've only recently moved. I live in a flat with a friend just up the road. By the way, I'm Julie.
JASON	I'm Jason.

(They look at each other for a few seconds. There is a special look between them)

JULIE	Are you the lucky man?
JASON	What do you mean, lucky man?

21

JULIE	The bridegroom?
JASON	Yeah, that's me.
JULIE	It must be very exciting – falling in love and getting married.
JASON	*(Unconvincingly)* Umm, very. I can hardly wait.
JULIE	What sort of buttonholes would you like?
JASON	I've no idea. I've never done anything like this before.
JULIE	There's a first time for everything. Let me show you what's on offer.

(Julie gets out her book)

Have a look through. *(They both look through book, Jason turns his eyes to Julie as she points out different buttonholes)* Have you seen anything you fancy?

JASON	*(Still looking at Julie)* Yes, I most certainly have.
JULIE	So which one is it then? *(Jason looks back into book)*
JASON	Actually, I'm not too sure. They're all very nice.
JULIE	*(Pointing to the book)* That's one of my favourites. *(Pause)* If you've any questions don't hesitate to ask.

(Jason looks through book)

JASON	Male or female?
JULIE	You've got me there, I don't think flowers have a gender.
JASON	No, I mean the friend you live with, male or female?
JULIE	Oh, I see. She's a girl I work with.
JASON	I'm so pleased. That's great.
JULIE	What's great?
JASON	*(Pointing to the book)* That rose, it's lovely. *(Pause)* Are you going out with anyone at the moment?
JULIE	No, I haven't met anyone I really like. *(Looking at Jason)* I'm sure when the right boy comes along, I'll know.
JASON	*(Looking into Julie's eyes)* Yes, it'll be plainly obvious.
JULIE	Is that what happened in your case?
JASON	*(Unconvincingly)* Not really. I mean, well, we just drifted together.

(Julie looks into book)

JULIE	So, which ones do you like?
JASON	I can't make up my mind.

22

JULIE	Why don't I leave the book? Then you can drop it into the shop when you've chosen.
JASON	Sounds good to me. So I'll see you Monday?
JULIE	Actually, I'm out on the van Monday making deliveries.
JASON	Now you've said that, I've just remembered. I'm a bit tied up Monday.
JULIE	Perhaps someone else can pop it round. *(Pause)* I really must be going.
JASON	Don't go yet. Let me get you a drink.
JULIE	Oh, all right. Could I have an orange juice, please?
JASON	You can have anything you want. *(Pause)* One orange juice coming up.
	(Jason pours two orange drinks)
JULIE	Have you known your fiancée long?
JASON	*(Looking fed up)* It seems like a lifetime.
	(Jason and Julie drink orange juice)
JULIE	In that case, you've obviously chosen the right girl.
JASON	*(Looking at Julie)* What makes you say that?
JULIE	I don't know. I just thought you must know her very well by now.
JASON	Where have you been all my life? I mean, tell me about your past.
JULIE	I wouldn't want to bore you with all the details.
JASON	It wouldn't be a bore. *(Unconvincingly)* I've always been fascinated with people's backgrounds.
JULIE	The last few years haven't been easy for my parents. My dad got made redundant, and then got into financial difficulties. Our house was repossessed. It nearly split their marriage. Anyway, they've moved up north, taking a live-in job with some wealthy aristocrat. So I decided to move here, and do my own thing.
JASON	I'm so pleased … I mean, I'm sorry to hear about your parents, but I'm glad you've moved here.
JULIE	It's a bit of a struggle, but I get by.
JASON	If there's anything I can do to help, please don't hesitate to ask.
JULIE	You'll be far too busy with all the excitement of married life.
JASON	I don't think so. *(Pause)* I've just had a brilliant idea. Are you going out tonight?
JULIE	No, I'm staying in.
JASON	In that case, I'll pop the book round to you later.

23

JULIE	You don't need to go to all that trouble.
JASON	It's no trouble. In fact, I've got nothing planned tonight.
JULIE	Well, if you're sure ...
JASON	Yes, I'm absolutely certain.
JULIE	All right, I'll see you later.

(Julie goes to hall exit)

JASON	Just a minute, I don't know where you live.
JULIE	How silly of me. Flat 2, 36a Brixham Way.
JASON	I know Brixham Way. See you about seven-thirty.
JULIE	Bye for now.

(Julie exits. Jason turns up the stereo. He has a broad grin across his face. He clenches his fist and punches the air)

JASON	*YES!!*

☜ *Curtain* ☞

ACT 1

⊘ *Scene II* ⊘

(As the curtain rises, the stage is empty and the doorbell is ringing. John enters from the kitchen and goes to the hall exit)

JOHN   *(Off)* Oh, hello, Stella, come in.

(John and Stella enter)

STELLA   Is Anne here?

JOHN   No, she's next door. Bill's borrowing my drill, he's too tight to buy one himself.

STELLA   So we're all alone.

(Stella moves close to John)

JOHN   Yes, I suppose we are.

(John moves away)

You've certainly put a lot of work into this wedding.

STELLA   I've planned everything meticulously. It's going to be a day this town will remember for ever.

JOHN   And how's Lucinda?

STELLA   She's just like her mum, ready, willing and able.

JOHN   I suppose when the wedding's over your life'll seem quite dull?

STELLA   That rather depends on you, John. *(Pause)* How have you been feeling since the other day?

JOHN   *(Looking puzzled)* OK, thanks. How about you?

STELLA   Suffering from night starvation, as usual.

JOHN   *(Smiling)* I know just the thing to make you relax.

(Stella moves close to John)

25

STELLA	What are you going to suggest, you little devil?
JOHN	A hot milky drink, just before bedtime. It always works with me.
STELLA	That's not quite what I had in mind. Still, we've both put our cards on the table. Shall we sit down?
JOHN	Yes, certainly. Make yourself at home.
	(John sits on sofa, and points to a chair for Stella)
STELLA	Thank you. *(Stella moves past chair and sits on sofa by John)* When did you first realise you wanted to try it?
	(Stella moves close to John)
JOHN	Try what?
STELLA	You know. *(Pause)* A 'new interest in life .... *RANDY!!*'
	(Stella puts her hand on John's knee)
JOHN	Oh that. Well with Jason moving out it seemed like a good idea.
STELLA	And to think I never suspected a thing.
	(Stella crosses her legs)
JOHN	It just seemed the right time. Although I'm a bit concerned about the divided loyalties.
STELLA	Let's face facts, we're all consenting adults.
JOHN	It's quite a commitment.
STELLA	Don't forget your motto. 'Enjoy each day to the full.'
JOHN	You're absolutely right. Plus the fact it'll be another way of keeping fit.
STELLA	I must be honest, that's something I've never considered.
JOHN	It's the affection I'm really looking forward to.
	(John gets up from the sofa to get a drink)
STELLA	That's what most of us are searching for.
JOHN	I can see myself now; romping about on the grass, on a spring day.
STELLA	Oh John, I'm not sure ...
JOHN	Do you know? People say that having a good licking is very therapeutic.
STELLA	You certainly don't suffer with any inhibitions, do you?
JOHN	There's nothing wrong with that.
STELLA	Of course not. It's just that it's been so long. *(Pause)* Things are moving much quicker than I expected. I'm feeling quite flushed.

26

JOHN	In that case you'd better have a drink.

(Stella rummages about in her handbag and gets out a bottle of perfume, she sprays it all over herself, then puts perfume back into handbag. John brings a drink and hands it to Stella)

I've filled it with ice, that'll soon cool you down.

(John sniffs)

What's that smell?

STELLA	It's *Stuck on you.*

(John looks at the bottom of his shoe)

JOHN	Is it? I can't see anything.
STELLA	No you silly boy, it's the name of my new perfume – *Stuck on You.* Don't you like it?

(John sniffs)

JOHN	Well, it's certainly different.
STELLA	It turns men wild, it brings out their animal instincts. Don't let's waste any more time with small talk.

(Stella lies back on sofa, lips puckered, arms apart, waiting for action. Anne enters)

ANNE	*(Looking at Stella)* Hello, Stella.
STELLA	Ahh ... *(Stella jumps up and runs to hall exit)* I must be going ...
JOHN	But I thought you'd come round to see Anne.
STELLA	I'll see you later.

(Stella exits to hall)

JOHN	That woman's cracking up. I reckon she's been on the bottle.
ANNE	I expect the wedding's getting to her. She's been so preoccupied with it.
JOHN	Well, it must be something, she's been talking rubbish. *(Pause)* I didn't realise you'd told her we'd be getting a dog.
ANNE	I haven't mentioned it to anyone.
JOHN	You must have, she even knew we're calling it *Randy.*
ANNE	Well, I can't remember saying anything. *(Anne looks at her list)* Right now, I've got to go to the supermarket.
JOHN	I'll come with you. I could do with a bit of fresh air.
ANNE	You can't, you're needed next door. When Bill plugged your drill in, it blew up!

27

JOHN	WHAT? That idiot destroys everything he touches. He's a walking disaster.
ANNE	I said you'd pop round and have a look at it.
JOHN	That's it. I'm not lending him anything else. *(Pause)* I suppose I'd better go and see what he's done.

(John exits to hall. Anne gets her handbag. Jason enters from hall)

ANNE	Hello, darling, had a good day at work?
JASON	Mum, we've got to have a serious talk.
ANNE	I can't stop now. I'm just off to the supermarket.

(Anne exits to hall, Jason paces up and down the room. The doorbell rings. Jason exits to hall)

JASON	*(Off)* Hello, Chris. Thank goodness you're here. *(Jason and Chris enter)* I've got to talk to someone.
CHRIS	Whatever's up? When you rang and said you'd got a problem I thought that …
JASON	I've just met the girl I'm going to marry.
CHRIS	I've driven here like a lunatic, to sort out some major crisis, only to be told of your wedding at which I'm the best man. *(Pause)* You prat.
JASON	No, you don't understand. I've fallen in love with a …
CHRIS	How sweet. Personally I'm not into all that love rubbish. As long as they can cook, clean and are clued up on the *Kama Sutra*, I couldn't care less.
JASON	I'm not marrying Lucinda. I'm in love with another girl.
CHRIS	You're having a laugh, aren't you?
JASON	I've never been so serious about anything. *(Pause)* Two days ago I met Julie.
CHRIS	Julie who?
JASON	She's from the local florist, she called round to sort out the buttonholes.
CHRIS	So what's that got to do with you calling the wedding off?
JASON	We looked through her book. *(Looking dreamy)* But I couldn't make up my mind, so I went to her flat, and when I gazed into her eyes …
CHRIS	Oh, I get it. Your head filled with romantic music, your eyes filled with stars and your heart went into overdrive, pumping blood to parts of your body that even beers can't reach.
JASON	Chris, I'm serious.
CHRIS	So am I. Now you listen to me. In five days you're marrying Lucinda. It's too late to change your mind.

28

JASON	I don't care if it's five days or five seconds. *(Shouting)* I'M CALLING THE WEDDING OFF!
CHRIS	I feel sorry for you both. You'll break Lucinda's heart; and her mum'll break your neck.
JASON	Whatever are we going to do?
CHRIS	We're not going to do anything. You've got yourself into this mess, you're on your own.
JASON	But we're best mates. We've been through everything together.
CHRIS	Don't start laying the guilt trip on me. *(Pause)* Have you given any thought to the consequences of all this?
JASON	Of course I have, and that's why we've got to sort things out.
CHRIS	Don't keep bringing up the word 'we'. When will you get it into your thick skull it's nothing to do with me?
JASON	So you're prepared to condemn me to a loveless marriage?
CHRIS	You should have played the field and got all this out your system years ago.
JASON	It's no good living in the past, we've got to ...
CHRIS	You've had plenty of chance to put it about. But you've always been far too serious.
JASON	None of this is helping my present predicament.
CHRIS	Why didn't you join the Club 18–30 as a rep? Then you could have partied till you reached the pleasure planet.
JASON	Lucinda's mum seemed to have my life organised. Before I knew it she'd got us engaged, and then wedding plans started creeping into the conversation.
CHRIS	Hang on. I've just had a brilliant idea.
JASON	Thank goodness for that. I knew you wouldn't let me down.
CHRIS	Emigrate to Australia.
JASON	Look. All I've got to do is tell Lucinda that I'm not going to marry her.
CHRIS	That you've fallen in love with another girl.
JASON	Yes.
CHRIS	And you've spent the last two days gazing into her eyes.
JASON	Yes.
CHRIS	She'll have to let the two hundred and fifty guests know, and send all the presents back. *(Speaking quickly)* Cancel the photographer, cars, vicar, caterers, orchestra, bar staff, and break the hearts of six bridesmaids.

29

JASON	Yes.
CHRIS	Best to emigrate.
JASON	Yes. I mean no.
CHRIS	Why don't you marry Lucinda and have your flower girl as a first reserve.
JASON	I'm *not* marrying Lucinda, and that's all there is to it.
CHRIS	What's wrong with her, she's got all the right bits, hasn't she?
JASON	Of course she has, but there's no sparkle when we're together.
CHRIS	You could always give her a squirt of Mr Sheen.
JASON	Lucinda'll make someone a lovely wife, but she's not the girl for me.
CHRIS	Look, you've only got to learn six words that'll guarantee marital success with any girl.
JASON	What six words?
CHRIS	Sorry darling, it's all my fault.
JASON	Haven't you ever had that incredible feeling when you're close to a very special girl and your whole body starts tingling?
CHRIS	What, you mean, when you fancy a bit of nooky?
JASON	No, I'm talking about being in love. In my wildest fantasies I never realised such feelings existed. But now I've found the girl of my dreams, I'm not letting her go.
CHRIS	This is all getting too heavy for me.
	(Doorbell rings. Jason exits to hall. Chris sits on sofa)
JASON	*(Off)* Lucinda, come in. Chris and I have got to have a talk with you.
	(Chris jumps off sofa and goes out kitchen exit)
LUCINDA	*(Off)* What? About the wedding arrangements?
	(Jason and Lucinda enter)
	Where's Chris?
JASON	I'll just get him. *(Jason looks around room, he tries to open kitchen door, but it won't open)* Chris, are you in there? Come out.
LUCINDA	What's going on? Are you two playing a joke on me?
JASON	It's certainly not a joke. Just bear with me. *(Jason hammers on door)* Chris, open this door.

30

(The door suddenly flies open and Chris runs out past Jason and Lucinda, pushing both of them out of the way as he exits to hall)

CHRIS   Must be going, it's been nice knowing you, Jason. Bye, Lucinda.

(Chris exits to hall, Jason runs after him)

JASON   Come back here, you coward. I thought you were my mate.

CHRIS   *(Off)* Will you leave me your stereo? Oh, and your watch?

LUCINDA   I knew it. He's getting nervous about being the best man. I said we should have chosen one of my friends from the *Young Farmers Club*.

JASON   Lucinda, we've got to have a serious talk about the wedding.

LUCINDA   That's good. Because I want to talk about the wedding vows.

JASON   What about the wedding vows?

LUCINDA   Mummy's told me not to say 'obey.'

JASON   But it's nothing to do with your mum. In any case something's happened that ... *(Doorbell rings)* Oh no!!

LUCINDA   Perhaps it's Chris come back for another game of hide and seek.

JASON   I knew he wouldn't let me down.

(Jason exits to hall)

SID   *(Off)* Hello, we're the video men.

(Sid enters pushing Alf in a wheelchair. Both are wearing 'film crew' caps, Alf is wearing sunglasses. Attached to one of the chair's handles is a vertical pole, with a flashing light at the top. Halfway down the pole is a spotlight. They also have a cassette player and video camera. Alf is holding another pole, with a microphone hanging from it. Jason enters)

               We're videoing your wedding. We've got a few details to sort out.

JASON   Oh. Well it's not convenient at the moment. Could we phone you later?

SID   It won't take long. In any case we're very busy people. Our card. *(Sid hands over a card to Jason. He looks at it)*

               (To Lucinda) Don't look so worried, dear, we'll guide you through it.

LUCINDA   I'm not worried at all. In fact, I'm looking forward to it.

(Alf, who is in the wheelchair, doesn't look too well, he's almost asleep. Sid walks around Lucinda, making a square with his hands and looking through it)

SID   Hmm, this could be difficult.

LUCINDA   What do you mean difficult?

SID   I'm trying to find your best side.

(He continues to move around Lucinda)

31

LUCINDA	I beg your pardon?
SID	You will be wearing a veil, won't you?
LUCINDA	Of course I will. Look, instead of wasting time chattering, we should be sorting out the details.
SID	You're right, we've got the blushing bride. *(Aside)* Now all we need is Dracula.
JASON	Have you videoed many weddings?
SID	Many weddings? You're talking to the professionals, mate. We're a household name in the video business.
JASON	But I thought you worked with my dad.
SID	Well yes, but that's just my spare-time job.
LUCINDA	*(To Sid)* What's the matter with your friend?

(Alf gets out of chair and unseen by Lucinda, he comes up behind her and puts his hands on her shoulders)

Ahh …

ALF	Don't be nervous, just relax, you'll be safe in our hands.

(Alf removes sunglasses. Lucinda jumps)

LUCINDA	You can walk! Why were you in that wheelchair?
SID	It's not a wheelchair, it's a dolly. Right, Alf. Let's show these good folks what we're going to do. Now you stand over there.

(Sid moves Lucinda to one side of the stage)

ALF	It's my turn to drive.
SID	OK. Keep your hair on. I'll go for a take. This'll get your adrenalin pumping.

(Sid switches on the lights then sits in the chair. Alf gets hold of the chair handles)

Walk slowly towards me. Everybody ready? QUIET! WEDDING TAKE ONE. ACTION!!

(Alf pulls chair backwards across stage. Sid holds camera to his eye and dangles microphone pole over Lucinda's head. Lucinda stands looking in amazement)

ACTION. ACTION. CUT! The shot's ruined. What's up with you?

LUCINDA	*(Looks amazed)* What do you mean? What was I supposed to do?
SID	That's the trouble, working with amateurs. Just walk towards me. *(Alf pushes chair back to starting place)* WEDDING TAKE TWO. ACTION. *(Lucinda follows chair as Alf pulls it backwards over Jason's foot, causing Sid to hit Lucinda's head with the microphone pole)*

32

JASON	
LUCINDA	Ahh ...

ALF   Whoops, sorry. *(He pulls chair off Jason's foot)*

SID   CUT! That's a wrap. *(Pause)* Don't tell me, I can see you're both impressed.

(Sid switches off the lights)

ALF   That's what we in the profession call mobile shots. *(Pause)* In church, you'll be following me, pulling Sid in this dolly.

LUCINDA   Are you suggesting that, in front of all the guests, I'll be walking down the aisle, following you, dragging that contraption, whilst your mate's hitting me on the head with that pole?

SID   You shouldn't have been so close.

LUCINDA   I'm not doing that, let's forget the ...

SID   This is really going to impress you.

(Sid has a cassette player attached to the chair. He puts on a tape of Billy Connolly telling a rude joke, followed by laughter)

That's going on your wedding tape.

LUCINDA   I'm not having people laughing at me as I walk down the aisle.

ALF   No, it's for the speeches, when someone says something funny. *(Alf starts to laugh)* It's called canned laughter.

LUCINDA   I think it's best if we forget the whole thing. We'll get someone else. You see, I don't ...

SID   When you're having the wedding photos taken I'll be walking around with the video camera hidden under my jacket.

(Sid puts video camera into his jacket with the lens poking out)

LUCINDA   Why would you want to do that?

SID   Background reactions. Things people wouldn't say to your face.

ALF   I normally hide behind the gravestones. Then people can't see me videoing them.

SID   You soon find out who your friends are. We've had some good laughs.

ALF   What, like when we videoed the best man saying the bride looked as fat as a barrel? *(Sid and Alf laugh)*

SID   She didn't speak to him again, after watching the video.

LUCINDA   I'm not having anyone videoed unless they're aware you're doing it.

33

SID	Why not? That spoils all the fun.
ALF	We'll put 'em at the end, in the out-takes.
SID	That's where we usually put some shots of the bride in her bra and pants.
LUCINDA	WHAT?
ALF	I normally visit the bride's bedroom before the wedding, to get a few intimate pictures.
SID	It's surprising how that boosts the tape sales.
LUCINDA	Oh no, certainly not! You're not videoing me half naked.
ALF	When you can't see us, WATCH OUT, 'cause Alf and Sid will be about.
LUCINDA	I'm not having that. Jason, tell them.
SID	Come on, Alf, we must be going.
ALF	See you on Saturday.
SID	Don't worry about a thing. Leave it all to us.

(Alf gets into chair and they exit to hall)

LUCINDA	I'm not having those idiots videoing my wedding.
JASON	Lucinda, we've got to talk about the wedding.
LUCINDA	Talk? I'm going home to talk to Mummy. We've got to hire a professional company.

(Lucinda exits to hall)

JASON	Come back, Lucinda. I don't want to get married.

(Jason sits on sofa and stares into space. John enters from hall with an electric drill)

JOHN	What's up with Lucinda? She's just zoomed off in her car as though she'd seen a ghost.
JASON	She's just met your two video mates.
JOHN	Oh good. I said they wouldn't let you down.
JASON	Dad, we've got to have a very serious talk.
JOHN	I'm sorry, but it's going to have to wait, that idiot next door has just blown up my electric drill.
JASON	But it just can't wait.
JOHN	Don't tell me you're worrying about your honeymoon. I'll explain everything later.

(John exits to kitchen)

JASON	DAD, WAIT, I NEED TO TALK NOW!

(Jason sits looking into space for a few seconds, doorbell rings, Jason exits to hall)

(Off) Julie! Come in.

(Julie and Jason enter from hall)

JULIE	Thank you for yesterday, I had a lovely time. *(Pause)* So what have you been at today?
JASON	I was just deciding what to pack.
JULIE	*(Looking sad)* I see, what, ready for your honeymoon?
JASON	No, I'm thinking of emigrating. It seems to be my only option, now I've met you.
JULIE	Oh dear. I think I'd better go.

(Julie walks to hall exit)

JASON	No, don't go. You're the only person making any sense at the moment.
JULIE	I don't want to cause you any more trouble.

(Jason walks over to Julie)

JASON	The last two days have been the best in my whole life.
JULIE	Oh, Jason, I was hoping you'd feel the same as me.

(They kiss. Jason puts his arms around Julie)

I never realised what love was, until I met you. I can't bear it when we're apart.

JASON	That's all I wanted to hear you say. Now I'm certainly not marrying Lucinda.
JULIE	What shall we do? I'm scared.
JASON	I'm not scared. *(Pause)* I'm petrified. I've got to talk to Lucinda and sort things out.
JULIE	Whatever will her mum say?
JASON	I don't think she'll say much. *(Pause)* She'll be too busy trying to kill me.
JULIE	Whatever happens, we'll face it together. *(They kiss)* Oh, Jason, I love you, so much.

(They kiss passionately)

REV. STEVENS	*(Off)* Hello, may I come in?

(Rev. Stevens enters from hall. Jason and Julie jump apart)

I'm sorry, but the door was open.

35

JASON	*(Looking embarrassed)* We were just …
REV. STEVENS	Yes, I thought you were. Please, let me introduce myself. I'm the Reverend Alan Stevens. Now, you must be Jason?
JASON	That's right, but where's our own vicar, the …
REV. STEVENS	And obviously this is the young lady you're very much in love with.
JASON	So where's the Reverend Hall?
REV. STEVENS	I've bad news for you. He's had a motorbike accident and broken both legs. He won't be able to marry you.
JASON	*(Jason hugs the Rev. Stevens)* That's wonderful!
REV. STEVENS	What, that the Reverend Hall's broken both legs?
JASON	No. I'm sorry. I mean … is he going to be all right?
REV. STEVENS	They've said he'll make a full recovery, but he's got to spend two weeks in hospital.
JASON	What perfect timing. I couldn't have planned things better myself.
REV. STEVENS	That's not quite the response I was expecting.
JASON	Let me explain. You see, I don't want to get married. It's all been a dreadful mistake.
REV. STEVENS	*(To Julie)* Oh dear, you must be devastated hearing all this.
JULIE	No, I'm just over the moon. *(Julie hugs the Rev. Stevens)*
REV. STEVENS	I'm getting very slightly confused here.
JASON	We've been looking for a way out, and now everything's falling into place.
JULIE	Thank you so much. *(Julie hugs the Rev. Stevens)* I could kiss you.
REV. STEVENS	Oh well, if you must. *(Rev. Stevens stands waiting for a kiss. Julie kisses him)* So are you both saying you want the wedding called off?
JASON	Yes, please. Oh, this is too good to be true. *(Jason goes to hug the Rev. Stevens but the Rev. Stevens kisses Julie instead)*
REV. STEVENS	You've certainly left things a bit late.
JULIE	We realise that, *(Julie hugs Jason)* but our future happiness depends on it.
JASON	You'll be condemning me to a lifetime of misery if you don't call it off.
REV. STEVENS	Well, if you're sure, we'd better make the arrangements.
JULIE	This is the best news I've ever had.

(Jason and Julie kiss passionately)

36

REV. STEVENS	Enjoys kissing, but doesn't want to marry. I've lost all contact with the youngsters of today.
JASON	Let's have a drink to celebrate.
REV. STEVENS	I thought we'd covered every eventuality in training college. But this is certainly a new one on me.
JASON	What would you like? Sherry, whisky, gin?
REV. STEVENS	Oh, no, I'm TT.
JASON	I beg your pardon?
REV. STEVENS	I only drink tea. *(Rev. Stevens gets a tea bag out of his cassock and hands it to Jason)* I carry a bag in case of emergency.
JULIE	Would you like me to make it?
JASON	Yes please, and make mine a large one.

(Jason hands tea bag to Julie, she exits to kitchen)

REV. STEVENS	Could I use the little room, please, only I've a slight bladder problem?
JASON	Yes. It's through that door, first right.

(Rev. Stevens exits to hall. Phone rings. Jason answers it)

Hello ... Hello, Jack ... Oh, right, so you've managed to get a kettle ... it just needs repairing ... I see ... well hang onto it, I think the wedding's off ... Yes, off ... I'll explain later ... bye.

(Jason puts down phone, doorbell rings)

What now? *(Jason exits to hall)*

(Off) Stella? Lucinda?

(Stella and Lucinda enter, followed by Jason)

What are you doing here?

STELLA	We're not having those stupid videomen. My little Lucinda's been in floods of tears.
JASON	Lucinda, you and I have got to talk.
STELLA	There's nothing to talk about, I knew I should have booked a professional company.

(Jason pushes Lucinda and Stella to hall exit)

JASON	Why don't you take your mum back home, and I'll be round in a minute?
STELLA	We're not going anywhere until I've sorted out this wedding video.
JASON	Lucinda, we've got to discuss the wedding. You see I ...

37

STELLA	Pop out to the Merc and get my mobile phone, dear. It's on the back seat. I'll soon book a competent firm.
	(Lucinda exits to hall)
	I don't know what your father was thinking of.
JASON	Why don't you have a word with him? *(Looking guilty)* He's in the bedroom.
STELLA	Is he? Right. We've got a few things to sort out.

(Stella exits to hall. Jason runs to kitchen just as phone rings. Jason picks it up)

JASON	Hello Jack ... Oh, so it's gone into redial mode ... Yes, the wedding's still off ... I've got to go ... I'll speak to you soon, ... bye.

(Jason puts phone down and runs to kitchen exit, just as Lucinda enters from hall with phone)

LUCINDA	Where's Mum?
JASON	She's in the bedroom with my dad. Why don't you join them?
LUCINDA	Pardon?
	(Loo flush off)
JASON	They're sorting out the wedding video.
LUCINDA	Oh, right. I'll pop up.
JASON	That's good. Take your time. I mean, we've had some more presents. Have a look at them.
	(Phone rings)
LUCINDA	Are you getting excited about the wedding?
JASON	You know me. The original Mr Cool. I'll just get the phone.

(Lucinda exits to hall. Jason answers phone)

	Not now Jack, I haven't got time ... Yes, take the kettle back and see if you can get a refund ... bye.

(Jason leaves phone off the hook. He runs to kitchen exit just as the Rev. Stevens enters from hall)

REV. STEVENS	What a blessed relief.
JASON	*(Walking over to Rev. Stevens)* Is that supposed to be a joke?
REV. STEVENS	Is everything all right?
JASON	Oh, yeah. Things couldn't be better. *(Pause)* Would you just bear with me for a minute?

(Jason runs to kitchen exit just as Stella enters from hall with her mobile phone)

38

STELLA	He's not up there.
JASON	*(Turning round)* Oh dear. I must have misheard what he said.
REV. STEVENS	Hello. I'm the Reverend Stevens.
STELLA	Stella Parsons. The bride's mother.
REV. STEVENS	You must be very proud of your daughter.

(They shake hands)

STELLA	Yes I am. *(Pause)* Where's the Reverend Hall?
REV. STEVENS	I'm afraid he's had a motorcycle accident. He's in hospital with two broken legs.
STELLA	The stupid man. So what's he going to do about my daughter's wedding?
JASON	I've just suggested we postpone it.
STELLA	WHAT? For one minute I thought you said postpone the wedding.
JASON	I did … er … as a sign of respect for the Reverend Hall.
STELLA	He's not dead, is he? I've never heard such rubbish.
REV. STEVENS	I really think we should let the youngsters decide. After all, they're the ones getting married.
STELLA	I'm telling you here and now, there's just no way that my daughter's wedding will be postponed.
JASON	But in the circumstances, it doesn't seem right.
STELLA	Don't be ridiculous, I'll phone the Bishop, and get a replacement.
REV. STEVENS	That won't be necessary. If the wedding goes ahead, I shall officiate.
STELLA	Oh. Well, I suppose you vicars are all the same. Just make sure you don't fluff your lines.

(Lucinda enters from hall)

REV. STEVENS	Hello. *(Stella tries to introduce Lucinda to the Rev. Stevens)*
STELLA	Of course you two haven't met, I'd like to introduce my dau …
JASON	*(Getting hold of Lucinda)* I don't feel too well. I need some fresh air. Let's go for a walk.

(Jason runs to hall exit, Lucinda pulls him back)

LUCINDA	Not until we've sorted out this wedding video.
JASON	I want to go now. Please come with me Lucinda.

STELLA	You've probably got pre-wedding nerves, sit down for a minute.
	(Jason starts to pace up and down room)
	I assume the Reverend Stevens will want to talk to you both.
JASON	Would anyone like a cup of tea? I'll go and get one.
	(Jason runs to kitchen exit)
STELLA	Nobody wants a cup of tea. Come back here.
REV. STEVENS	I'd still like mine, please.
LUCINDA	Jason, whatever's up with you? You're like a cat on hot bricks.
	(Jason runs over to Lucinda)
JASON	I must talk to you, Lucinda. Let's go somewhere private.
	(Jason pulls Lucinda to hall exit)
REV. STEVENS	I'm sorry, but I'm very confused.
JASON	That makes two of us.
REV. STEVENS	Is the wedding on, or is it off?
STELLA	ON!
JASON	OFF!
STELLA	ON!
	(Lucinda pulls Jason back into room)
LUCINDA	Whatever's going on? Where's the Reverend Hall? *(To Stella)* Mummy, why did Jason say the wedding's off?
STELLA	The Reverend Hall can't take the service, he's broken his legs.
REV. STEVENS	It was a motorcycle accident.
STELLA	He shouldn't have been riding the thing. *(Pause)* I suppose he's another of these men going through the mid-life crisis.
LUCINDA	So, who's taking the service?
REV. STEVENS	If the wedding goes ahead, I shall officiate.
STELLA	There's no 'if' about it, the wedding will go ahead.
JASON	Isn't it time you went home and got Reg some dinner?
STELLA	Are you trying to get rid of me?
JASON	*(Getting hold of Lucinda's hand)* I must talk to you. It's very important. Come with me. *(Jason pulls Lucinda to hall exit. Julie enters from kitchen with three cups of tea on a tray)*

40

JULIE	I've made the tea.
REV. STEVENS	Ah, now we can sort everything out.

(Jason lets go of Lucinda, runs over to Julie, takes tray, gives it to Stella then pulls Julie to the hall exit. Everyone looks on in amazement)

JASON	Come on, Julie. *(Pause)* Lucinda. I'm sorry. The wedding's off!

(Jason and Julie exit. Stella drops tray on floor. It makes a loud crash)

∽ *Curtain* ∽

ACT II

∞ Scene I ∞

(As the curtain rises, Lucinda is sitting in a chair. She is clutching Jason's photo and crying pathetically. Stella is pacing up and down the room and Anne is sitting in another chair staring into space)

TELLA   So you're telling me you've no idea where he is?

NNE   He's not been in contact. His bed's not been slept in. I'm worried.

UCINDA   *(Crying)* What's going to happen, Mummy?

(Stella walks over to Lucinda and puts her arms around her)

TELLA   I'll tell you what's going to happen. When I get my hands on that boy, I'll do things that'll bring tears to his eyes.

NNE   I don't think we should lose our tempers. We're all a bit upset at the moment.

TELLA   And to think my Lucinda could have had the pick of any boy she wanted.

UCINDA   *(Crying pathetically)* I just want my Jason. *(Looking at photo)*

TELLA   Why she had to choose a no-hoper like your son, I'll never know.

NNE   Hang on a minute. I'm not having you talking about Jason like that.

TELLA   It's the truth. *(Pause)* Or have you a plausible explanation why he ran off with that girl?

NNE   Well, I don't really …

TELLA   He's broken my Lucinda's heart. He's got to pay for that.

(Lucinda cries loudly)

NNE   He obviously needed time to decide about getting married.

TELLA   We're three days away from the wedding. Don't you think he's left it a bit late?

NNE   I suppose he should have sorted things out before.

42

STELLA	That Reverend Stevens knew more than he was letting on.
ANNE	I'm sure there's a simple explanation to all this.
STELLA	The simple explanation is, your irresponsible son's run off with some girl who's supposed to supply flowers, not personal services to the bridegroom.
LUCINDA	*(Wailing)* Ahh ... where is he, Mummy?
STELLA	*(Stella pats Lucinda's head)* There, there, Lucy Lou, don't worry.
LUCINDA	Why doesn't he ring?
	(Stella gets very cross)
STELLA	Ring, I'll ring his bleeding neck!
LUCINDA	*(Lucinda blows her nose)* Brrr ... I can't stop crying.
STELLA	I'll make him understand that no-one, but no-one, messes with me. *(Pause)* I suppose I should have guessed. They say 'like father, like son.'
ANNE	What do you mean by that?
STELLA	I wasn't going to say anything. I was hoping he'd lose interest.
ANNE	Lose interest?
STELLA	Your husband's not happy with just one woman. He can't keep his hands off me.
ANNE	*What?*
STELLA	Ask him. Whenever he's around, he's always trying to force himself on me. It's so embarrassing.
ANNE	I don't believe it. You must be mistaken.
STELLA	I happened to mention that Reg goes out Fridays and your husband's eyes lit up like spotlamps.
ANNE	What, you mean he ...?
STELLA	Yes, he said he'd be straight round and it wasn't the nine o'clock news he was hoping to turn on.
ANNE	You can't be talking about John.
STELLA	I certainly am. Ask him about the photo he's stolen of me, topless on holiday.
ANNE	This is all too much. They're both at it. The lecherous louts!
STELLA	Of course, I didn't succumb to his advances. Fortunately I'm used to dealing with frustrated men. But a lesser woman may have fallen foul.

(John enters from kitchen)

43

JOHN	Is there any news?
ANNE	Yes. You've been trying it on with Stella. *(Anne walks over to John and slaps his face)*
JOHN	Ouch! *(Pause)* What are you on about? I'm not that desperate!
	(Stella slaps John's face)
	Ouch! ... That hurt.
ANNE	And to think I've given you the best years of my life.
STELLA	I can see you have.
	(Anne looks at Stella then slaps John's face again)
JOHN	Ouch! ... Will you two stop hitting me.
ANNE	You gigolo! You're nothing but a wolf in sheep's clothing.
JOHN	Have you gone completely mad?
ANNE	I must have been mad to marry you. And to think Jason's going to be just the same.
JOHN	I hope he is. He's my son and I'm proud of him.
ANNE	You know what I mean. He's not happy with one woman.
JOHN	Have you two been hitting the bottle?
STELLA	Where's my photo? I expect it's already faded where you've been drooling over it.
JOHN	What photo?
STELLA	Friday nights – mean anything? Who's begged to come round for a drink, and whatever else is on offer whilst Reginald's out?
ANNE	It's pitiful for a man of your age. Next you'll be wearing a dirty old raincoat.
JOHN	I haven't got a clue what you're talking about.
STELLA	Typical of a man. Deny everything, thinking he'll get away with it. You've got the hots for me.
JOHN	I'm not even lukewarm when you're around.
STELLA	Just listen to him. Butter wouldn't melt in his mouth.
JOHN	I don't know what's going on, but I can assure you there's been a misunderstanding.
STELLA	Don't come the innocent. Only the other day on that very sofa you were fantasizing over some perverted acts.
JOHN	For the last time, will you listen to me? I haven't done anything.

44

ANNE	So are you telling me you've not made advances to Stella?
JOHN	Of course I haven't. The thought's never crossed my mind.
STELLA	He's bound to say that. He's hardly going to admit that he finds me sexually irresistible.
LUCINDA	What about me, Mummy?
JOHN	I haven't been anywhere near your daughter either.

(Doorbell rings)

ANNE	We'll sort this out later. I've got far too much on my mind at the moment.
JOHN	And I always thought a man was innocent until proved guilty.

(John exits to hall)

(Off) Hello, Fred. Come in.

(John and Fred enter from hall)

FRED	Hello all. I hear young Jason's chickened out. When are we getting our presents back?
LUCINDA	Stop them, Mummy. They're all laughing at me.

(Stella goes over to Lucinda and puts her arms around her)

STELLA	No-one's laughing at you, dearest. *(Looking into room)* Not if they've got any sense.
LUCINDA	What shall I do? What's going to happen to me?
STELLA	You're getting married in three days, just as we've arranged.
FRED	Who's she marrying then?
STELLA	*(Calmly)* She'll be marrying Jason, of course.
FRED	But he's run off with another girl.
LUCINDA	Mummy, stop him. *(Pathetically)* Why have you forsaken me, Jason?
FRED	You should phone a dating agency and see if they can find a last minute replacement.
STELLA	Suggestions like that are in very poor taste, Mr Stubble.
FRED	I was only trying to be helpful.
STELLA	That's the sort of help we can do without.
FRED	When the wife left, I joined a dating agency. They kept sending me thirty-year-old girls, it was lovely!
STELLA	*(Looking bored)* How very interesting.

45

FRED	They crossed me off their books for lying about my age. I'd told them I was thirty-five.
ANNE	You men are all the same.
FRED	Any chance of a drop of gin?
ANNE	The glasses are in the kitchen. They'll need washing. *(Looking at John)* Well ... off you go.

(John exits to kitchen)

STELLA	I'll check with Reg to see if there's any news.

(Stella picks up a piece of paper, then speaks into a CB microphone)

Ice Maiden to *Road Hog*, have you got your ears on?

ANNE	What on earth's that?
STELLA	It's a CB. If I press this button I can talk to Reg. He's given all his drivers a picture of Jason and he's offering a thousand pounds reward to the man who apprehends him.
ANNE	Anybody would think a murder's been committed.
STELLA	There's still a chance that could happen.

(Stella speaks into CB microphone and reads from piece of paper)

Ice Maiden to *Road Hog*, have you got your ears on?

FRED	*(Looking at Anne)* That's CB talk. It's what the truckers use.
STELLA	Reg has given me a list of CB phrases, so that I can talk to the drivers, to find out if they've seen Jason.
FRED	I used to have a CB till some *Good Buddy* smashed my rig for chatting up his wife.
ANNE	This is all very unnecessary. I'm sure Jason'll be home soon.
FRED	Yeah, but will it be in time for his wedding?
LUCINDA	Ahh ... *(Lucinda blows her nose)* I'm already on my fourth box of tissues.
FRED	Last night in the pub, they were having bets on whether the marriage would take place. I could make a few quid.
LUCINDA	Ahh ... I'll never be able to show my face at the *Young Farmers* again.
STELLA	I just need five minutes alone with your son. I'd soon make him realise his responsibilities.
ANNE	Please, Stella. Let's try and remain calm, so that we can sort things out.
STELLA	*(Speaking into CB microphone)* *Ice Maiden*, anyone for a copy.
VOICE ON CB	*Ice Maiden*, you've got the *Road Hog*, you're hitting me wall to wall.

46

STELLA	*(Speaking into CB microphone)* That's a big ten four. Have you seen Jason, *Good Buddy*?
VOICE ON CB	Negatory, but will keep on trucking, Roger Dee, over and out.
ANNE	What are they talking about?
STELLA	They've not found him yet, but they're still looking.
ANNE	Why don't they talk plain English?
FRED	It's to confuse the police.
ANNE	Why bother? The police get confused if you ask them the time.

(Stella puts down microphone and John enters from kitchen with glasses and pours out drinks)

JOHN	Here you are, Fred.
STELLA	I'll have a sherry. It might help to settle my nerves.
ANNE	And me. I've got a hot flush coming on.
JOHN	*(Aside)* Not another power surge. *(Pause)* Lucinda?
LUCINDA	I couldn't drink a thing. I just want my Jason back.

(John hands round drinks)

FRED	Cheers, everyone! *(Fred holds up glass)* The bride and groom. *(Pause)* Wherever he may be.
LUCINDA	Ahh ... Mummy. He's making fun of me.
STELLA	Mr Stubble. Please think what you're saying.

(They all drink. Doorbell rings)

FRED	That could be Jason, forgotten his key.
JOHN	I'll go.

(John exits to hall)

(Off) You'd better come in. You've upset Lucinda and her mum.

(Lucinda jumps out of her chair and runs to hall exit)

LUCINDA	He's come back, I knew he would. Jason ...

(John enters, followed by Sid carrying a video camera and Alf carrying a microphone tied onto a pole)

Oh no, Mummy, it's those horrid videomen.

SID	What's up then? Hasn't the wanderer returned?
ALF	Perhaps he's not ready to start his life sentence!

47

(Sid nudges Alf, they both laugh)

STELLA	I don't find your stupid remarks at all funny.
SID	We could always video the divorce for you. All part of the service.
STELLA	I've been desperately trying to hire a professional company, but they're all booked up.
ALF	There's no need to take it out on us just because your daughter's been dumped.
LUCINDA	Mummy ... have I been dumped?
JOHN	I'm sure Sid and Alf will make an excellent job of videoing the wedding.
FRED	That's if there is one!
JOHN	Who'd like a top up?

(John goes around with the drinks)

STELLA	These should have been the happiest days of Lucinda's life. But thanks to your stupid son, she's facing the world on her own.
LUCINDA	Why's he left? What's wrong with me?
SID	It's not your fault. *(Aside)* Mother Nature's got to take some of the blame.
ALF	Jason shouldn't have gone off like that. He was totally out of order.
STELLA	That's the first intelligent thing you've said.
ALF	Well, I mean, if he don't turn up, we'll have to cancel the stag-night.
SID	This is serious. We've got that erotic dancer coming, with her pet python.
ALF	We can't cancel that, we'll have to carry on without him.
SID	Yeah, we'll drink to absent friends.
STELLA	My daughter's sitting there breaking her heart, and you're worried about a stupid stag-night.
SID	We were lucky to get Lusty Linda. Her pet python should be paid a fortune for what he has to do.
ALF	*(Aside)* I'd do it for nothing.
STELLA	It's difficult to believe that morons like you are part of the human race.
ALF	Strikes me Jason had a lucky escape from having you as a mother-in-law.
JOHN	Drink up, everybody. Here Stella let me top you up.

(John goes over to Stella with sherry bottle)

LUCINDA	Will I be wearing my wedding dress on Saturday, Mummy?

48

ALF	Of course you will. *(Pause)* You can put it on when you go to the chippy for your dinner.
SID	I've heard he's emigrating.
ALF	I bet he's on some beach with that bird, having a snog.
LUCINDA	Stop them, Mummy. This is all getting too much for me to bear.
ALF	Still, every cloud's got a silver lining. *(Pause)* It's happy hour at the 'Nag's Head' Saturday. You'll be able to drown your sorrows for half the price.
STELLA	That's it, I've had just about enough of this.
ANNE	What lovely weather we've been having lately.

(Stella gets cross)

STELLA	I'll never forgive your pathetic son, as long as I live.
JOHN	Please, Stella. Let's try and remain calm.
STELLA	Lucinda could have married any young farmer she wanted.
ALF	One thing's for sure, she'd have been quite at home feeding the pigs.
LUCINDA	That's done it, Mummy. I can feel the tears welling up.

(Lucinda starts crying again)

STELLA	How dare you.
ANNE	I believe the forecast is good for the next few days.
STELLA	If only Lucinda had chosen someone more suited to our lifestyle.
JOHN	Are you trying to say that Jason's not good enough.
STELLA	You couldn't possibly deny there's a difference in their upbringing. And that explains why that rotten maggot son of yours couldn't face up to his responsibilities.
SID	You were right, John, when you said she was a jumped-up tart.
STELLA	I beg your pardon?
SID	John only said the other day, if it wasn't for your husband's money, you'd be making a living on the streets.
STELLA	WHAT! How dare you! Take that!

(Stella throws drink at Sid)

ANNE	Mind you, these weathermen never get it right.

(Alf defends himself with the microphone pole)

49

ALF	Don't get your knickers in a twist.
STELLA	*(Stella kicks Alf. He starts hopping around room)* You pea-brained oaf.
ALF	Ahh ... That hurt. You vicious old bag.

(Stella grabs the mayor's picture from the sideboard and smashes it over Alf's head. The picture finishes up with Alf's head poking through it)

STELLA	Oh dear. I've just shattered the mayor's work of art.
ALF	Sod the mayor. You nearly shattered my brains.
LUCINDA	Mummy, please. *(Lucinda is still crying. The Rev. Stevens enters from hall)*
FRED	*(Trying to hold Stella)* Calm down, Stella.
REV. STEVENS	Hello, everyone. Goodness me. *(Nobody spots the Rev. Stevens)* Stop, children, please stop.

(There is a bell on sideboard which the Rev. Stevens picks up and rings loudly)

We must love one another.

(Everybody stops fighting and looks at Rev. Stevens. Alf removes picture and throws it on sideboard)

STELLA	Hello, Vicar. How nice to see you.

(Stella brushes Fred off. A photo falls from his pocket)

REV. STEVENS	You've dropped a photo, Mr Stubble. *(Rev. Stevens picks up photo and looks at it. Then he has another close look)* It's you, Mrs Parsons. Um ... you're almost overexposed.
STELLA	I beg your pardon?
REV. STEVENS	The photo, you're well-developed. I mean, what natural colour.
STELLA	*(Looking at photo)* It's my holiday snap. What are you doing with it?

(Stella snatches photo and puts it into her handbag)

FRED	It ... er ... must have fallen into my pocket the other day.
REV. STEVENS	I've just called to see what's happening about the wedding.
ALF	What wedding's that, Vicar?
LUCINDA	That's it, I'm off again. *(Lucinda starts to cry again)*
REV. STEVENS	Is there any news?
ANNE	Not yet. But I'm sure there will be.
REV. STEVENS	Should I cancel the choir, and tell the organist?

STELLA	No. Just iron your cassock and make sure your organ's working. The wedding's going ahead as planned.
REV. STEVENS	Just supposing Jason hasn't returned by then? What are …?
STELLA	Reverend Stevens, I'm telling you, and everybody here, Jason will marry Lucinda. Even if they have to take him up the aisle in a straitjacket.
REV. STEVENS	Let's hope that won't be necessary.
STELLA	I've spent the last year organising my daughter's wedding, and it's not being ruined by some irresponsible bridegroom. Come on, Lucinda, let's go.

(Lucinda gets up still whimpering. Stella glares at Sid and Alf)

	I'll see you all at the church. On Saturday.
FRED	Let's hope Jason turns up.
STELLA	If he doesn't turn up for his wedding, I'll still see you in church for his funeral.

(Stella and Lucinda exit to hall, followed by Anne)

SID	Her husband deserves a medal. *(To Rev. Stevens)* May I give you our card, Vicar?

(Sid gives Rev. Stevens a card)

REV. STEVENS	Thank you.
SID	From the cradle to the grave. We can help you relive life's treasured moments.
ALF	Stereophonic sound's extra. But we knock off the V.A.T. for cash.

(Anne enters room)

ANNE	Would you like a cup of tea, Vicar?
REV. STEVENS	No, thank you. I just popped in for a progress report.
ANNE	I'd better have your phone number in case we hear anything.
REV. STEVENS	Well … um … I'm out most of the time. I'll ring you tomorrow. *(Pause)* Goodbye.

(Rev. Stevens exits to hall)

ANNE	What are we going to do? I've never seen Stella so angry.
ALF	I'll have a bruise on my leg. *(Alf pulls up his trousers and puts his leg on sofa arm. He starts rubbing his leg)* I might do her for GBH.
SID	She really went berserk. This was one of me best shirts. Look at it now.
ALF	I don't fancy your Jason's chances when Stella gets hold of him.

51

ANNE	I just want him to come home, so we can sort things out.
SID	Why don't you put an advert on the local radio?
ALF	Yeah, they're always finding missing dogs.
SID	*Missing, Jason, slipped his lead, friendly and ready to be mated. If found before Saturday, take him to the church. If found after Saturday, put him in the dog-house.*

(Sid, Alf and Fred laugh)

ANNE	It's nothing to laugh about. Whatever does he think he's playing at?
FRED	He'll come back when he's ready. I must be going. I've promised to help at the 'Nag's Head.'

(Fred walks to hall exit)

SID	We'll come with you.
ALF	I could do with a brandy, purely for medicinal purposes.

(Alf rubs his leg)

SID	You will let us know what's happening, won't you? Only our services are in great demand.

(Sid, Alf and Fred exit to hall)

ANNE	I'll never be able to show my face again.
JOHN	Don't worry. Things are never as bad as they seem.
ANNE	No, I suppose you're right. I mean the fact that Stella spent thousands of pounds, plus the last year organising the grandest wedding this town's ever seen, and our son, who happens to be the bridegroom, decides to do a last minute disappearing act. It's no big deal!
JOHN	Now you've put it like that, when I get my hands on Jason, I'll kill him!
ANNE	I owe you an apology for thinking you fancied Stella. When Fred dropped her photo, I realised what had happened.
JOHN	He's certainly one for the girls. And Stella desperately craves affection.
ANNE	If they ever get together, it'll be like a wrinklies' version of Romeo and Juliet.
JOHN	I'm going to check my roses. It might help me relax.

(John exits to kitchen. Anne tidies up room)

VOICE ON CB	*Road Hog* to *Ice Maiden*, have you got your ears on?
ANNE	*(Looking around room)* Pardon?

VOICE ON CB	*Road Hog* to *Ice Maiden*, have you got your ears on? Come back.
	(Anne walks over to the C.B. and looks at it)
	I've got an eyeball on Jason, shall I give him a good slapping?
ANNE	No, don't do that. Leave the boy alone.
VOICE ON CB	*Ice Maiden*, come back.
	(Anne grabs CB and piece of paper, she presses button on CB)
ANNE	This is *Ice Maiden* to *Road Hog*. *(Looking at paper)* That's a negatory, don't hurt him..
VOICE ON C.B.	That's a big ten four. He's heading home. I'll call off the truckers.
ANNE	That's good. *(Looking at paper)* I mean, that's a big Roger Dee, over and out.
	(Anne puts down CB, runs to kitchen exit and shouts from door)
	John, come here quickly.
	(John enters)
JOHN	Whatever's wrong?
ANNE	*Road Hog*'s said Jason's on his way home. Oh, I'll explain later. *(Doorbell rings)* That's probably him.
	(Anne exits to hall)
	(Off) Stella, Lucinda.
	(Anne, Stella and Lucinda enter)
STELLA	I've forgotten my CB. *(Pause)* Is there any news?
ANNE	*(Looking suspicious)* Um … No, not a thing. We've just been sitting here talking. *(Looking vague)* About the … weather.
STELLA	I'll give Reg another call, to see if there's been any sightings.
	(Stella gets hold of C.B.)
ANNE	No, you musn't do that. *(Pause)* He's just called and … said … umm … he'd gone for a tea break.
STELLA	Oh … all right. I'll try him later.
	(Stella puts CB in her handbag)
LUCINDA	Do you think Jason will come back, Mummy?
STELLA	Of course he will, darling, if he wants to carry on living.
ANNE	We must go to the supermarket, John.

53

JOHN	*(Looking vague)* Sorry?
ANNE	The supermarket, you know we were just going to get the shopping.
JOHN	What? ... Oh yes, sorry to rush you, Stella.
ANNE	We'll let you know the minute we hear anything.

(Doorbell rings)

Oh, no ... How's Reg been keeping?

STELLA	I beg your pardon?
ANNE	Your Reg. He's such a hard-working man, is he keeping well?
STELLA	Yes, thank you, although he'll be a lot better when we've sorted out this wedding.
ANNE	Ah, yes, the wedding.
JOHN	When we got married, it rained all day. We all looked like drowned rats. The photographer's camera was full of water.

(Doorbell rings again)

STELLA	How very interesting. Aren't you going to answer the door?
ANNE	Just going. John, why don't you show Stella and Lucinda your roses.
JOHN	Oh yes. Come with me, they're out in full bloom.

(John beckons Stella and Lucinda to kitchen exit)

STELLA	We haven't got time now.

(Stella and Lucinda walk to hall exit. Anne runs in front of them)

ANNE	Are you sure? John said they'll definitely win first prize at the flower show.
STELLA	*(Unconvincingly)* I'm so thrilled for you.
JOHN	I've got a hundred quid bet riding on them.

(Doorbell rings again)

STELLA	Would you please let us out and that persistent bell pusher in.
ANNE	I think I'm going to have a nervous breakdown.
STELLA	I suggest you have it after we've gone.

(Anne exits to hall)

ANNE	*(Off)* Oh, it's you. Come in.

(Anne and Chris enter)

What a lovely surprise, it's Chris, I'm so pleased to see him. He's such a good friend of the family.

(Anne kisses Chris, he looks surprised)

STELLA	Have you heard anything?
CHRIS	No. I just called to see if you'd got any news.
STELLA	Are you sure, you're not hiding anything?
LUCINDA	Don't get on at Chris, Mummy. It's not his fault.
STELLA	Umm … these boys are all the same. It's probably got something to do with their upbringing.
ANNE	I'm sure Chris would tell us if he knew anything.
STELLA	I wouldn't bet on it.
ANNE	Well, we mustn't hold you up, Stella.
STELLA	No, I must be going. I've got to co-ordinate the search.
ANNE	Keep us informed if you hear anything.
JOHN	Bye, Stella, Lucinda.

(Stella and Lucinda go to hall exit. Doorbell rings)

ANNE	Good grief, this is like Russian Roulette.
STELLA	It would probably save time if I answered the door.

(Stella exits to hall and returns holding Jason by the ear)

Look what I've found. *(Looking very angry)* Before you have a chance to make one of your speeches, let me tell you and everyone here, you will be marrying my Lucinda on Saturday. Make no mistake about that!

❧ *Curtain* ❧

55

ACT II

∞ Scene II ∞

(As the curtain rises, Anne is walking around room and John is sitting in a chair)

ANNE   It should have been the happiest day of his life. He never smiled once. *(Pause)* He was forced into it and it's all your fault.

JOHN   Amazing, isn't it. If anything goes wrong, it always turns out to be my fault.

ANNE   You should have stopped the wedding. You're his father, you could have done something.

JOHN   What, like shoot the vicar?

ANNE   Don't be stupid. You should have sorted something out.

JOHN   Not even an Act of God would have stopped it.

ANNE   Jason only got married because he couldn't let Lucinda down on her big day.

JOHN   I think the fact that Stella was going to kill him had some bearing on his decision.

ANNE   He was in an impossible situation.

JOHN   It was the grandest wedding I've ever been to. The whole town was at a standstill. Even the mayor was impressed.

ANNE   I heard Stella telling *him* that Reg goes out Friday nights.

JOHN   I'll say one thing for Stella. Where men are concerned she never gives up.

ANNE   At least you're off her hit list now, after stinking out the church with rotting manure.

JOHN   How was I to know that idiot farmer would deliver it fifteen minutes before the wedding, blocking our car up the drive.

ANNE   You should have put your wellies on. Or at least taken your suit off.

JOHN   There wasn't time. I was sweating when I'd finished.

ANNE   You don't have to tell me. I was in the fall-out zone.

JOHN	Still, at least I had plenty of room when I was eating my meal.
ANNE	What are we going to do about Jason?
JOHN	It's too late now. He's made his vows, for better or for worse.
ANNE	I feel sorry for him. He won't have that 'special feeling' you get when you're first married.
JOHN	What 'special feeling'?
ANNE	I should choose your next words very carefully. They could be your last.
JOHN	Don't get me wrong – I'm happy enough. *(Pause)* Well, for a married man.
ANNE	I can't believe I'm hearing this.
JOHN	All I'm saying is that as the years pass, it can get a bit monotonous.
ANNE	What are we talking about? Your performance in bed? Because that's just about as exciting as watching paint dry.

(Doorbell rings. John exits to hall)

JOHN	Saved by the bell. *(Off)* Hello, Fred, come in.

(John enters, followed by Fred wearing earrings)

FRED	It's a sad time for Jason, losing his freedom. It must be a black day for the boy.
ANNE	What makes you men think that you're doing women a favour by marrying them?
JOHN	Yes, well, umm … what did you think of the reception?
FRED	It was all very nice. Well, as far as I can recall.
JOHN	Fred, you're wearing earrings. *(Pause)* They're a bit over the top, aren't they?
FRED	Actually they're not mine. I'm looking after them for a lady friend I met at the wedding.

(Anne looks closely at the earrings)

JOHN	So who's this mystery woman?
FRED	I can't remember. I'd sunk a lot of beer by the end of the day. Everything was a blur.
ANNE	They look very familiar.
FRED	I was on my way home. It was so dark I couldn't see a thing. Anyway, I came across this woman. She was well slaughtered.

JOHN	Most of the guests were. That was probably because the drink was free.
FRED	We were just having a bit of a snog, when suddenly she went into overdrive. I think she may have bruised me tonsils. Here, come and have a look. (*Fred opens his mouth widely. John has a look in*)
ANNE	All right, Fred, we get the picture.
FRED	She gave me her earrings so we could get down to some real serious ...
ANNE	I don't think we want to hear any more.
JOHN	Speak for yourself. I do. Tell us exactly what ...
ANNE	And you've no idea who it was?
FRED	No, it was pitch-black. In any case I was well shot away.
ANNE	So why are you wearing them?
FRED	I'm trying to find their rightful owner.
ANNE	I think that's a very responsible attitude, Fred.
FRED	Actually, I couldn't care less who owns them. I just want another snog, now I'm sober. It's about time I had a bit of female company to spice up my life.
JOHN	Fred, come and have a look at my roses. They're ready for the flower show next week. I'll be walking off with first prize.

(*Fred and John exit to kitchen. Anne tidies up. The phone rings, Anne picks it up.*)

ANNE	Hello ... Oh hello, Bill, ... thank you very much, he'll be pleased. I'll pop round with him. I've got some photos to show you ... see you in a minute ... Bye.

(*Anne puts down phone and continues tidying up. Doorbell rings, Anne exits to hall*)

(*Off*) Hello, Stella, come in.

(*Stella and Anne enter*)

STELLA	What a day, it was definitely the best wedding this town's ever seen.
ANNE	It all went very well. I should think you were very pleased.
STELLA	I just couldn't believe she was my little girl.
ANNE	I must say Lucinda looked lovely.
STELLA	Like a princess, waiting for her knight in shining armour.
ANNE	I thought the bridesmaids were sweet.
STELLA	My Lucinda was like a pure white angel, ready to ascend into Heaven.
ANNE	The choir sang well, no sign of laryngitis.

STELLA	My Lucinda was like a film star. I'm surprised no-one asked for her autograph.
ANNE	The weather couldn't have been better.
STELLA	My Lucinda was like a beauty queen who'd just won the title.
ANNE	Would you like a coffee?
STELLA	My Lucinda looked like … Oh, no thank you.
ANNE	I expect you're glad it's all over.
STELLA	The wedding may be over, but people will talk about it for years. All the local papers were there. Did you hear the interview on the radio?
ANNE	No, I'm afraid we were fighting our way through manure at that point.
STELLA	The mayor's invited me for drinks next week. He's introducing me to our local MP.
ANNE	I'm so pleased for you. *(Pause)* It was very kind of you to pay for the honeymoon.
STELLA	Think nothing of it. They'll enjoy Scotland. I wanted them to go abroad, but Lucinda doesn't like flying.
ANNE	What time are they travelling?
STELLA	Their train leaves at two-fifteen this afternoon. It was far better for them staying locally last night.
ANNE	You shouldn't have booked them into the Grand. It's so expensive.
STELLA	Reg uses it all the time for his business clients.
ANNE	I've never been in there.
STELLA	We treat it like a second home. I've told Lucinda to mention my name. That'll keep them on their toes.
ANNE	You must be very pleased with everything.
STELLA	We've had a few unnecessary hiccups, but it's been a fairy tale ending. I suppose you could say I'd organised the perfect wedding.
ANNE	I'm pleased to see that success hasn't gone to your head.
STELLA	Of course, you can't hold me responsible for those two imbeciles who videoed the wedding.
ANNE	I thought they did very well.
STELLA	If I never see either of them again, it'll be too soon.
ANNE	I'm sure you'll be pleased with the tape.

STELLA	That's most unlikely. *(Pause)* You didn't find any earrings at the reception, did you? I seem to have lost mine.
ANNE	Were they *(Anne gives a description of earrings Fred is wearing)*?
STELLA	Yes, how did you know?

(Fred and John enter from Kitchen)

JOHN	Hello, Stella.
ANNE	*(To John)* Bill rang, we've got to slip next door for a minute.
JOHN	What does he want to borrow now?
ANNE	He doesn't want anything. He's got a special feed for your roses. Apparently it's used by professional growers.
JOHN	Oh … I've always said he was a good bloke.

(Anne picks up some wedding photos, then looks at Stella)

ANNE	Let's pop round and get it. Fred'll look after you Stella.

(John and Anne exit to hall)

STELLA	Did you enjoy the wedding, Mr Stubble?
FRED	I certainly did, how about you?
STELLA	It was like a dream come true. *(Pause)* You're wearing earrings. *(Stella looks very closely)* Where did you get them?
FRED	At the reception, someone gave them to me to look after.

(Stella removes earrings from Fred's ears)

STELLA	These are my earrings.
FRED	Oh!! *(Pause)* So you were the girl I met on my way home.
STELLA	Good grief, it's all coming back to me.
FRED	It was so dark I didn't recognise you.
STELLA	I seemed to be in a daze, I was just floating along on a cloud.

(Stella puts earrings in her handbag)

FRED	I'm not surprised, the amount of drink you'd put away.
STELLA	I gave you the earrings to look after. Then we …
FRED	Er … yes … we did, didn't we? Well I never, what a funny old world it is.
STELLA	I hope you don't think I was throwing myself at you?
FRED	You certainly know how to Rock and Roll.
STELLA	I beg your pardon?

60

FRED	I was watching you on the dance floor. You looked lovely at the wedding. You're like a bottle of wine. *(Pause)* You improve with age.
STELLA	Thank you, Fred, you're a real gentleman.
FRED	You'll be lonely without Lucinda.
STELLA	Yes. And Reg is always working.
FRED	He shouldn't leave a good-looking woman like you on her own.
STELLA	Oh, Fred. *(Stella gets close to Fred)* You say the nicest things.
FRED	I've just bought a CB. I call myself *Silver Fox*, why don't you pop round and see it.
STELLA	Reg goes out Friday nights. I get so bored on my own.
FRED	Come round this Friday and I'll show you my equipment.
STELLA	I'll be there. *(Stella gets her handbag)* I've got something for you. *(Stella gets out her holiday photos)* Here, it's yours. *(Stella hands Fred photo)*
FRED	*(Looking at photo)* I'll put it under my pillow, it'll warm me up on cold winter nights.
STELLA	I've just had a thought. Reg has just got himself a very lucrative continental contract.
FRED	Oh, that's nice.
STELLA	No, you're missing the point. He'll soon be away several days travelling through Europe. You'll be able to come over to my house. We're very private.
FRED	Sounds good to me.
STELLA	I thought after Lucinda left, life would be dull, but it looks as though it's on the up again.
FRED	Yeah, you could be right. I've managed to get a few of them Viagra pills.
STELLA	I've always fancied the more mature man.
FRED	Youngsters haven't got the monopoly on life's sensual pleasures. It's just that we're built for comfort and they're built for speed.
STELLA	I'm all for a bit of slow cruising.
FRED	I suggest you fasten your seat-belt, I'm already firing on all cylinders.
STELLA	*(Getting hold of Fred's hand)* Oh, Fred. Thank you for bringing some life back into my life.

(They start to kiss. Doorbell rings. Fred puts photo in his pocket)

FRED	Oh damn. I'll go. *(Fred exits to hall)*
	(Off) Hello, Sid, Alf.

STELLA	Oh no, I don't believe it.

(Sid, Alf and Fred enter, Sid has videotape and camera, Alf has a microphone)

SID	It's a masterpiece! Although I say it myself, it's absolutely brilliant.

(Sid holds up videotape)

	Fades and wipes, camera angles correct. Superb editing. Stereophonic sound. Still, we won't bore you with all the technical details.
ALF	We've worked through the night. I've given it my all. I'm completely drained.
SID	How many copies do you think you'll want?
STELLA	I'm not sure, I'll need to see it first. *(Aside)* Thank goodness we've got lots of photos.
SID	There won't be any illegal pirates, will there?
STELLA	*(Looking confused)* I beg your pardon?
SID	We own the copyright. Additional tapes must be supplied by us.
STELLA	If you say so. *(Aside)* I shouldn't think we'll be wanting any.
ALF	Has anybody heard what happened to the best man?
FRED	It's unlike Chris. He's normally so reliable.
STELLA	I knew he couldn't do the job. I told them he wasn't up to it.
FRED	There wasn't any sign of him all day. I wonder whatever made him disappear like that?
STELLA	He probably couldn't face up to his duties. Making a speech would be difficult for someone like him.
SID	Poor old Jason looked completely lost.
STELLA	He should never have chosen that Chris. I knew he wasn't suitable for such an auspicious occasion.
ALF	Who was the boy you got to stand in?
STELLA	One of Lucinda's young farmer friends, he's got innate breeding.
ALF	Is that catching?
STELLA	There's certainly no chance of you getting it.
ALF	That's good. *(Looking at Sid)* You can't be too careful nowadays.
STELLA	I thought his wit and charm really made the day.
ALF	I suppose he's one of them yippies.
SID	You mean yuppies, Alf.

ALF	Yeah, that's what I said.
FRED	Had Jason ever met him before the wedding?
STELLA	No, he went straight from boarding school to university. Now he's into organic farming.
ALF	He should be careful messing about with things like that. It ain't natural.
FRED	I will say he did very well.
SID	Perhaps Chris thought the wedding would be cancelled if he didn't turn up.
STELLA	He should have realised what I start I always finish.
ALF	I enjoyed the reception.
STELLA	*(Unconvincingly)* I'd like to say it was a pleasure having you.
ALF	It was good in that tent.
STELLA	I assume you're referring to the marquee?
ALF	That band was good. I'm sure some of them blokes could read music.
STELLA	They could all read music. They're a professional orchestra. *(Pause)* I'll tell John you're here.

(Stella exits to hall)

SID	Her Reg didn't say a word at the reception. He was like a fish out of water.
ALF	I caught him on video, phoning one of his drivers. During the vicar's prayers.
SID	They say he's a workaholic.
FRED	He certainly doesn't enjoy socialising, and a little bird's told me he's lost his libido.
ALF	Was it valuable? Because he could always claim off his insurance.
FRED	I was on about his testosterone levels.
ALF	*(Looking vague)* Yeah, so was I.
SID	I'd like to find out who let the tyres down on our dolly. It ruined all our mobile shots.

(Stella enters from hall)

STELLA	They're just coming.
SID	I see the place next to you is for sale. I've always fancied living in a country cottage.
STELLA	*(Aside)* Thank goodness it's way above your price range.

(John and Anne enter from hall, John is carrying a container)

JOHN   That's the first thing he's ever given me. Hello, Sid, Alf. I won't be a minute, I've got to get this feed on my roses.

(John exits to kitchen)

ALF   It's a wrap.

ANNE   I beg your pardon?

ALF   It's in the can.

ANNE   I'm sorry, Alf, you've lost me.

STELLA   They've finished the video.

SID   It'll probably bring tears to your eyes.

STELLA   *(Aside)* I'm sure it will.

ALF   We've worked non-stop to get it finished.

SID   We'll be able to relax tonight. I fancy going to the 'Nag's Head'.

ALF   Your husband certainly enjoyed himself the last time he was there. He had a real good night with that erotic dancer.

ANNE   Erotic dancer?

ALF   At Jason's stag-night, didn't he tell you?

ANNE   He hasn't said anything.

ALF   They were like a double act. *(Pause)* By the time he'd finished, she was as naked as a jaybird.

FRED   He only did it to try and cheer Jason up. *(Aside)* Shut up.

ANNE   Is there anything else I should know?

ALF   If you've got a spare hour, I'll fill you in on all the juicy bits.

(Phone rings, Anne answers it)

ANNE   Hello … Good grief! … Oh no!

(Anne puts down phone and runs through kitchen exit)

STELLA   What was all that about?

ALF   Perhaps it was that erotic dancer asking John to join her act.

FRED   Will you shut up about her. Are you trying to get John hung?

ALF   Have I said something wrong?

FRED   Oh, no. You should have videoed them. Then Anne could have watched every explicit detail.

64

| ALF | I never thought of that. |

(Anne enters helping John in, he is clutching the watering-can with both hands and he looks numb)

| ANNE | Sit down, you'll be all right in a minute. |
| SID | Whatever's up with him? |

(Anne sits John down in a chair, he is still clutching watering can)

ANNE	He's just sprayed weedkiller over his prize winning roses.
ALF	What did he do that for? It won't do them any good.
ANNE	Bill, next door, got the packets mixed up, he gave John weedkiller by mistake. *(To John)* Let go of the watering-can, dear.
JOHN	I'll kill him. He did it deliberately.
ANNE	Don't be so stupid, of course he didn't.

(John gets up out of chair and goes to hall exit)

| JOHN | Why have we been lumbered with the neighbours from hell? I'm going to blow his house up. |
| ANNE | John, come here. |

(Anne pulls John away from door and tries to remove watering-can from his hands)

	It was an accident.
JOHN	I'm going to the garden centre tomorrow.
ANNE	It's too late to get any roses for the show now.
JOHN	No, I'm buying some ten-foot conifers to plant all down our boundary. If he wants war, he can have it.
ANNE	I'll get you a drink.

(Anne sits John back down still holding watering-can. Anne pours a drink and gives it to John)

| | Here you are. |

(John puts watering-can down and has a drink)

JOHN	I can't believe it. My head's thumping.
ANNE	Oh dear. It could be a bit of blood pressure. *(Pause)* Caused by Lusty Linda's naked body.
JOHN	Who's Lusty Linda?
ALF	I've just told your missus about that erotic dancer, and her pet python.
JOHN	You've lost me.

65

ANNE	Sorry dear, am I making things too complicated for you. I'M TALKING ABOUT THAT STRIPPER YOU ASSISTED IN GETTING STARKERS.
ALF	The one you said you'd like to ...
JOHN	Thanks Alf, I owe you. *(Pause)* It was just a bit of harmless fun.

(John has another drink)

SID	Would you like us to video your roses in all their magnificent splendour?
ALF	Before they all drop dead.
JOHN	Well, I suppose it's better than nothing.
SID	Right, leave it to us.

(Sid and Alf exit to kitchen, walking like two undertakers)

JOHN	My head's a bit better now.
ANNE	Don't speak too soon, the pain could return.

(Anne picks up a large vase)

JOHN	There's no need to be like that.

(Jason and Lucinda enter from hall. Lucinda looks lovely. She is now very self-confident and talks without her lisp)

This is just not my day.

JASON	Are you all right, Dad?
ANNE	Yes, he's all right. He's just sprayed his ... Jason! Lucinda!

(Anne puts down vase)

STELLA	WHAT ARE YOU DOING HERE? You should be at the station.
ANNE	Jason, why aren't you on honeymoon?
FRED	Perhaps he's had enough of married life already.
JASON	That's just it, we're not married.
ANNE } STELLA }	<u>WHAT?</u>

(Stella drops down onto sofa)

ANNE	Is this your idea of a joke? Because if it is I don't find it at all funny.
JASON	It's not a joke, Mum, we don't understand what's going on either.
STELLA	How can you say you're not married? That doesn't make any sense. *(Getting hysterical)* Two hundred and fifty people were at your wedding. We've got dozens of photos; I watched you sign the register.

66

LUCINDA	Mum, I know all this. If you remember, I was the bride.

(Stella gets up and starts to pace up and down the room)

STELLA	This is a nightmare. Please tell me I'm dreaming.
FRED	Just calm down a minute Stella, we'll soon …
STELLA	Calm down! What do you mean calm down?
JOHN	Let's find out what's going on. Jason, tell me exactly what's happened?
JASON	After the reception we went to the hotel.
LUCINDA	At breakfast this morning the manager gave us this note.

(Jason removes a piece of paper from his pocket and reads it)

JASON	*Please return home immediately, you are not married. I will explain everything at eleven-thirty* and it's signed the Reverend Stevens.
LUCINDA	The manager told us the note was left by a vicar.
ANNE	Why would he leave a note saying you're not married?
JOHN	If you don't get to the station soon, you're going to miss your train.
LUCINDA	There's no point going on honeymoon if we're not married.
FRED	She's quite right. It's bad enough if you are married.
ANNE	And you didn't see the Reverend Stevens?
JASON	No. He'd left before we'd got up.

(Reverend Stevens enters)

REV. STEVENS	Hello, I'm glad you're all here.

(Stella runs over to the Rev. Stevens and grabs him)

STELLA	What do you mean by telling my daughter she's not married?
REV. STEVENS	If you'd just bear with me, I'll explain everything.
STELLA	This had better be good. Your life depends on it. *(Stella lets go of Rev. Stevens)*
REV. STEVENS	I knew Jason didn't want to get married.
JASON	Who told you that?
FRED	*(Aside)* He probably had a message from God.
REV. STEVENS	I also knew Stella wouldn't cancel the wedding.
STELLA	You seem to be well informed. But that doesn't explain anything.
REV. STEVENS	I had to do something. How could I let my best friend marry the wrong girl?

67

JASON	Best friend? *(Rev Stevens removes wig, glasses, collar and cassock)* <u>CHRIS</u>!
LUCINDA	I can't believe it.
STELLA	Good grief!
ANNE	Whatever's going on?
FRED	Now I've seen everything, including a reverend being defrocked.
CHRIS	When Jason and I were young we made a pact. If either of us was in trouble, the other would do anything to help.
STELLA	So what's this stupid pact got to do with my daughter's wedding?
CHRIS	Jason was desperately trying to stop the marriage.
JASON	I'd begged Chris to help me.
CHRIS	I'm sorry, Lucinda, but I had to do something, so I decided to become the Reverend Stevens.
STELLA	You'll be sorry all right, you'll be very sorry.
ANNE	I don't understand any of this.
CHRIS	After Jason told me about Julie, I went home. My mum's church warden and she'd just had the news about the Reverend Hall breaking his legs.
STELLA	It won't be just your legs I'll break, it'll be every bone in your body.
CHRIS	That's when I had this flash of inspiration.
STELLA	You'll have a flash of my hand round your head any minute.
LUCINDA	Mum, for once in your life, please be quiet.
CHRIS	I decided with the Reverend Hall in hospital, I'd take his place.
ANNE	Take his place? What are you talking about?
CHRIS	Vicars are like policemen. The uniform gives them an air of authority, which makes people listen.
FRED	That's quite true. Last week a copper got my full attention when he threatened to book me, for speeding.
CHRIS	Anyway, I got a wig and cassock and dressed up. I was hoping to convince Lucinda that the marriage was a mistake.
JASON	But when you got here, she'd already left.
CHRIS	Yes, I saw you with Julie. Then I knew I had to stop the marriage.
JASON	I never recognised you.
CHRIS	That's when I realised I could get away with it.

STELLA	I've had enough of this silly chatter. I'm phoning the police. *(Walking to the phone)*
FRED	Hang on a minute, Stella. Let the boy finish.
ANNE	So why didn't they send a proper vicar?
CHRIS	Mum was dealing with the arrangements. I intercepted her calls from the Dean's office.
STELLA	May God forgive you, I certainly won't!
CHRIS	I'd convinced everyone that I was the replacement vicar sent to officiate.
JOHN	So why go ahead with the wedding?
CHRIS	Because I realised I couldn't stop it. *(Pause)* Stella wanted a magnificent wedding; she had one. Jason didn't want to be married; he isn't.
STELLA	You've made a mockery of the sanctity of marriage.
CHRIS	You're wrong. I've prevented a mockery from taking place.
STELLA	I suppose you think you're clever. Let me assure you, you're going to pay for this.
JASON	How did you know what to do?
CHRIS	As a choirboy I'd watched dozens of weddings.
	(They all stand silent for a few seconds)
LUCINDA	So we're *not* married?
CHRIS	No, I'm sorry Lucinda, you're not.
STELLA	You're in big trouble, boy. Impersonating a vicar is a very serious offence. I'm phoning the police. They'll lock you up and throw away the key.
	(Stella picks up phone)
LUCINDA	No, Mum, don't do that.
	(Lucinda puts phone down)
STELLA	Why ever not? What's up with you, Lucinda?
LUCINDA	I'm pleased we're not married, it would never have worked.
STELLA	Have you gone completely mad?
LUCINDA	Yesterday, I realised the marriage was a mistake. We spent all last night talking.
ANNE	*(Looking at John)* This is all your fault, you should have explained about the birds and the bees.
JASON	It's got nothing to do with the birds and the bees, but it's got everything to do with being in love.

69

LUCINDA	Mum, I've spent my whole life living in your shadow. Now I'm going to do my own thing.
STELLA	This is all too much for me. How can I ...?
FRED	I think your daughter's just grown up, Stella. It's time to let her go.
LUCINDA	Jason, I'll always look on you as the brother I never had.

(Lucinda kisses Jason)

CHRIS	*(To Lucinda)* I'm sorry, it was never my intention to hurt you. Perhaps we could have a drink some time?
LUCINDA	I'd love that. Jason's very lucky having such a good friend.
CHRIS	I think he's crazy to finish with such a gorgeous girl.

(Chris stands by Lucinda. They look into each other's eyes)

STELLA	I'm not feeling very well. It's all going to start again with another one of these no-hopers.

(Sid and Alf enter)

SID	Hello, Chris. *(To Jason)* Why aren't you two on honeymoon?
JASON	It's a long story, but we're not married.
ALF	Yes you are. We've got it all on video.
JASON	Chris made a guest appearance as the vicar.
CHRIS	Because I married them, they're not married.
ALF	I don't understand any of that.
SID	Don't strain your brain, Alf. *(Pause)* What about our video?
STELLA	Throw it in the bin where it belongs. *(Stella hands over video)*
SID	But we've spent hours getting it ready. It's probably the best one we've ever made.
STELLA	You keep it. I certainly don't want it.
SID	*(To Lucinda)* When you find the right boy, don't forget to let us know. We're the professionals.
LUCINDA	I'll bear that in mind. *(Lucinda looks at Chris)*
STELLA	I don't ever want to see you two clowns again. *(Pause)* I've never been so humiliated in all my life.
FRED	Calm down, Stella. It could have been worse.
STELLA	Are you joking? I've just organised the biggest marriage that never was.
JOHN	Look on the bright side. One day you'll be able to do it all again.

CHRIS	Mum phoned the bishop's office this morning and told them what I'd done.
STELLA	I feel positively sick. Whatever will the mayor say? I'll be a laughing stock.

(Doorbell rings. John exits to hall)

JOHN	*(Off)* Hello, you'd better come in.

(John and Julie enter)

JULIE	Hello, Jason, why aren't you on your honeymoon?
JASON	Because I'm not married.
JULIE	Aren't you? *(Looking happy)* You're not? Oh, that's wonderful ... I mean ...
CHRIS	That's why I left you the message to call round. *(Pause)* Jason'll explain everything.

(Julie talks to Jason)

LUCINDA	I hope you'll be very happy together.
JASON	Thank you.
LUCINDA	I've just had a brilliant idea. *(Looking at Chris)* What are you doing this week, Chris?
CHRIS	Nothing really ... why?
LUCINDA	Come to Scotland with me now. There's a first class hotel booked and waiting. I need to get away for a while.
CHRIS	What! ... I mean ... I'd love to.
LUCINDA	Come on then. Let's go and get you packed, or we'll miss the train.
STELLA	But you can't. You're a married ...
LUCINDA	No I'm not, Mum. *(Giving Stella a hug)* Thanks for a lovely wedding, even if I didn't get married ... Bye.

(Lucinda holds hands with Chris and they run to hall exit)

STELLA	I'm not feeling very well. *(Phone rings, John answers it)*
JOHN	Hello ... Yes, I'll get him ... Sid, it's your wife.

(John hands phone to Sid, he talks in background)

JULIE	Why are all those reporters out the front?
ANNE	They must have found out what's happened.
STELLA	This isn't the sort of publicity I was looking for.
JOHN	I think this is one wedding we'll never forget.

(Sid puts down phone)

SID   My wife said the phone's not stopped. We've had television companies, video shops, lots of townsfolk, all wanting copies of the wedding tape.

STELLA   That's just typical. Why can't people mind their own business?

(Sid holds up video tape)

SID   This little baby's going to be a big earner for us. *(Sid puts his arm on Alf's shoulder)* We'll never be able to thank you enough, Stella.

STELLA   Thank me? What for?

SID   If it hadn't been for your daughter's reception, I wouldn't have seen that cottage next to you is for sale.

STELLA   What are you getting at?

SID   Well, when we've sold all your wedding videos, we'll have enough money to put a deposit on it. Looks like we're going to be neighbours.

STELLA   WHAT! I CAN'T TAKE ANY MORE.

(Sid and Alf walk over to Stella to shake hands. She faints) Ahh ...

(Stella collapses into a chair. Anne, John, Fred, Sid and Alf try to revive her)

JASON   *(To Julie)* Will you marry me?

JULIE   I'd love to. *(Pause)* On one condition. Let's make absolutely certain that Chris is the best man this time.

(Jason and Julie kiss passionately)

∽ *Curtain* ∽

72

13 Dec 06

To Bob,
Very many thanks for all your help with my plays. Best wishes

Ray Hopkins

IT MUST BE LOVE
Raymond Hopkins

Farcical Comedy   ISBN:- 185205 257 0   M6 F4

Jason Taylor, a quiet unassuming person, is one week away from marrying Lucinda, his childhood sweetheart. The overzealous bride's mother, Stella Parsons, has turned the wedding into a personal crusade. No expense has been spared and a year's preparations have all come together to make it the event of the decade. Lucinda, who has always been dominated by her mother, has gone along with the lavish arrangements. As the wedding looms ever closer, everything is on track. That is, until Julie, a girl from the local florists, calls at the Taylors' to make some final arrangements. By a twist of fate, Jason is at home alone. Their inevitable first meeting sparks off that magical chemistry which makes two people fall hopelessly in love. From that point on, the plot twists and turns in a frantic manner, making the wedding a far more memorable occasion than even Stella could have imagined. Another hilarious play by the author of the highly successful LOVE BEGINS AT FIFTY.

LOVE BEGINS AT FIFTY

M3 F6   ISBN: 185205 229 5

A modern farce in two acts by Raymond Hopkins

SOME PRESS OPINIONS

This is one of the most frenetically funny farces I have reviewed for some time, up to the standards of the best of Ray Cooney ... side-splitting laughter ... a fast and furious farce which provides hilarious opportunities.

THIS WAS ONE OF THE SUMMER SHOWS IN TORQUAY IN 1999 WHERE IT PLAYED TO RECORD-BREAKING AUDIENCES THROUGHOUT A THREE MONTHS' RUN

SEND FOR OUR CATALOGUE OF OVER 300 TITLES

HANBURY PLAYS

Keeper's Lodge, Broughton Green, Droitwich
Worcestershire WR9 7EE
01905 23132 – Phone and Fax